Code Of Canon Law

Canon 66 «The Christian economy, therefore, since it is the new and definitive Covenant, will never pass away; and no new public revelation is to be expected before the glorious manifestation of our Lord Jesus Christ." Yet even if Revelation is already complete, it has not been made completely explicit; it remains for Christian faith gradually to grasp its full significance over the course of the centuries.

Canon 67 Throughout the ages, there have been so-called «private» revelations, some of which have been recognized by the authority of the Church. They do not belong, however, to the deposit of faith. It is not their role to improve or complete Christ's definitive Revelation, but to help live more fully by it in a certain period of history. Guided by the Magisterium of the Church, the sensus fidelium knows how to discern and welcome in these revelations whatever constitutes an authentic call of Christ or his saints to the Church.

Christian faith cannot accept "revelations" that claim to surpass or correct the Revelation of which Christ is the fulfilment, as is the case in certain non-Christian religions and also in certain recent sects which base themselves on such "revelations."

The Full of Grace:

The Early Years.

The Merit.

Joseph's Passion.

The Blue Angel.

The Boyhood of Jesus.

Follow Me:

Treasure with 7 Names

Where there are Thorns, there also will be roses

For Love that Perseveres

The Apostolic College

The Decalogue

The Chronicles of Jesus & Judas Iscariot:

I See You As You Are

Those who are Marked

Jesus Weeps

Lazarus:

That Beautiful Blonde

Flowers of Bounty

Claudia Procula:

Do You Love the Nazarene?

The Caprice of Court Morals

Christian Tenets:

On Reincarnation

Mary of Magdala:

Ah! My Beloved! I Reached You At Last!

Lamb Books
Illustrated adaptations for the whole family

LAMB BOOKS
Published by Lamb Books, 2 Dalkeith Court, 45 Vincent Street, London SW1P
4HH;
UK, USA, FR, IT, SP, PT, DE

www.lambbooks.org

First published by Lamb Books 2013
This edition
001

The author and publisher are grateful to the Centro Editoriale Valtoriano in
Italy for Permission to quote from the Poem of the Man- God by Maria Valtorta,
by Valtorta Publishing

Set in Bookman Old Style R
Printed and bound by CPI Group (UK) Ltd, Croydon, CR0, 4YY

The **Chronicles** Of
Jesus & **Judas**
Iscariot

Those Who Are Marked

LAMBBOOKS

Acknowledgements

The material in this book is adapted from 'The Poem of the Man+God' (The Gospel As Revealed To Me) by Maria Valtorta, first approved by Pope Pius XII in 1948, when, in a meeting on February 26th 1948, witnessed by three other priests, he ordered the three priest present to "Publish this work as it is".

In 1994, the Vatican heeded to the calls of Christians worldwide and have begun to examine the case for the Canonization of Maria Valtorta (Little John).

The Poem of the Man God was described by Pope Pius' confessor as "edifying". Mystical revelations have long been the province of priests and the religious. Now, they are accessible to all. May all who read this adaptation, also find it edifying. And through this light, may Faith be renewed.

Special Thanks to the Centro Editoriale Valtortiano in Italy for permission to quote from the Poem of the Man God by Maria Valtorta, nick named, Little John.

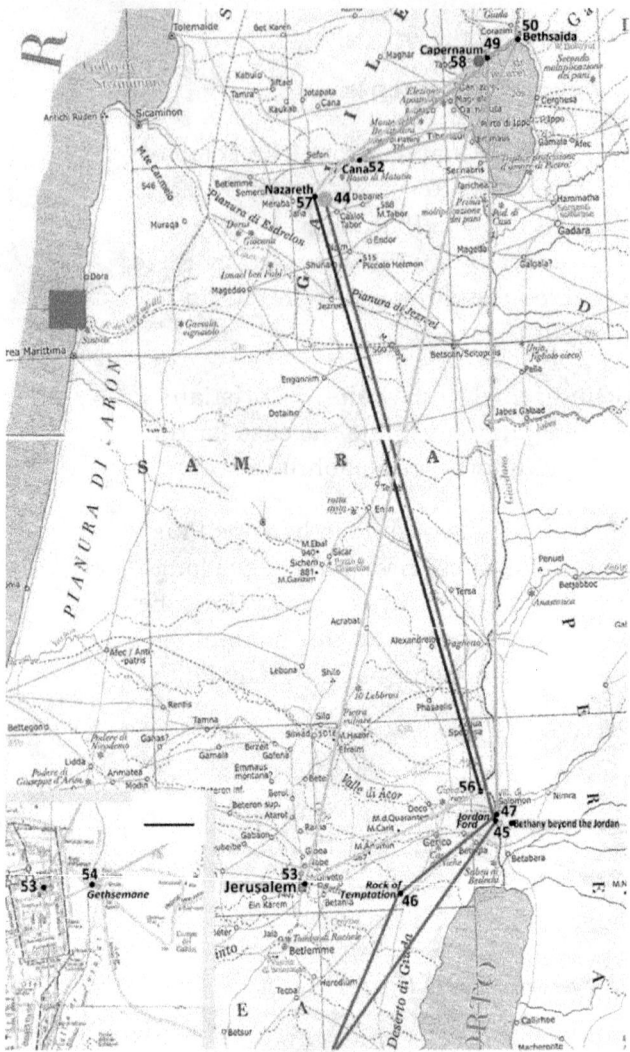

Jesus Goes To The Hotel In Bethlehem And Preaches From The Ruins Of Anne's House.

It is early on a bright summer morning and little thin strips of pink cloud, like brush strokes, paint the sky like strips of frayed gauze on a turquoise carpet.
Birds, exhilarated by the bright light, fill the air with the songs of Sparrows, blackbirds and redbreasts that whistle, chirp and brawl over a stem, a worm or a twig they want to take to their nests, to eat or on which to roost.

Swallows with rust coloured tops dart from the sky down to the little stream to wet their snow white breasts, refresh themselves in the water and catch a little fly still asleep on a little stem and then dart straight back up into the sky in a flash like a burnished blade, all the while, chattering joyfully.

Along the banks of the stream, two blue headed wagtails, dressed in pale ash- grey, walk gracefully like two little dames; holding up their long tails adorned with little velvet black spots. They stop to look with satisfaction at their beautiful reflections in the water before resuming their walk whilst a black bird, a real rogue of the wood, scoffs at them, whistling with its long beak.

In the thick foliage of a wild apple-tree growing all alone by the ruins, a nightingale calls her mate insistently, only becoming silent when she sees him coming with a long caterpillar wriggling in the grip of his thin beak. Two city pigeon escapees from a dove-cot that now dwell in the freedom of a crevice in a ruined tower, give vent to their effusions of love; the male cooing seductively for the benefit of the modest female.

With His arms crossed, Jesus, looks at all the happy little creatures and smiles.
'Are You already ready, Master? 'asks Simon, from behind Him.
'Yes, I am. Are the others still sleeping? '
'Yes, they are. '
'They are young... I washed Myself in that stream... The water is so cold that it clears the mind... '
'I'll go and wash now. '

While Simon, wearing only a short tunic, is washes himself and then puts his clothes on, Judas and John come out. 'Hail, Master, are we late? '
'No. It is only daybreak. But now be quick and let us go. '
The two get washed and put on their tunics and mantles.
Jesus, before setting off, picks some little flowers which have grown between the crevices of two stones, and puts them into a small wooden box that already contains other items; 'I will take them to My Mother...'He explains. ' She will love them... Let us go. '
'Where, Master? '
'To Bethlehem. '
'Again? I do not think the situation is a favourable one for us... '
'It does not matter. Let us go. I want to show you

where the Magi came and where I was. '

'In that case, listen. Excuse me, will You, Master?
But let me do the talking. Let us do one thing. In
Bethlehem and at the hotel, let me speak and ask
questions. You Galileans are not awfully liked in
Judaea, and much less here than anywhere else.
Nay, let us do this: your clothes show that You and
John are Galileans. It's too easy. And then... your
hair! Why do you persist in wearing it so long?
Simon and I will change mantles with you. Simon,
give yours to John, I'll give mine to the Master.
That's it! See? You already look a little more like
Judaeans. Now take this. 'And he takes off the
cloth covering his head: a yellow, brown, red, green
striped length of material, like his mantle, held in
position by a yellow cord, he places it on Jesus'
head, adjusting it along His cheeks to hide His fair
hair. John puts on the very dark green one of
Simon. 'Oh! That's better now. I have a practical
sense. '

'Yes, Judas, you have a practical sense. That is
true. Watch, however, that it does not exceed the
other sense. '

'Which one, Master? '

'The spiritual sense. '

'No! No! But in certain cases it pays to be more a
politician than an ambassador. And listen... be
good a little longer... it is for Your own good... Do
not contradict me if I should say something...
something... which is not true. '

'What do you mean? Why tell lies? I am the Truth
and I want no lies in Me or around Me.'

'Oh! I will only tell half lies. I will say that we are
all coming back from remote places, from Egypt for
instance, and that we are seeking news of dear
friends. I will say that we are Judaeans coming
back from exile. After all, there is some truth in
everything, and I will be speaking, and... one lie

more, one lie less... '
'But Judas! Why deceive? '
'Never mind, Master! The world lives on deceit. And
at times deceit is a necessity. Well: to make You
happy, I will only say that we are coming from far
and that we are Judaeans. Which is true for three
out of four of us. And you, John, please do not
speak at all. You would give yourself away. '
'I will be quiet. '
'Then... if everything works out all right... we shall
say the rest. But I do not believe it... I am shrewd, I
grasp things at once. '
'I see that, Judas. But I would prefer you to be
simple. '
'It does not help much. In Your group, I will be the
one in charge of difficult missions. Let me carry on.
'Jesus is reluctant. But He gives in.
They set out, walking first around the ruins and
then along a massive windowless wall from the
other side of which comes braying, mooing,
neighing, bleating and the queer cry of camels.
They follow an angle in the wall and emerge onto
the square of Bethlehem with fountain at its
centre. The shape of the fountain is still slantwise
as it was on the night of the visit of the Magi but
across the street where the little house that on the
same night had been bathed in the silvery rays of
the Star, there is now only a large gap strewn with
ruins, surmounted by the little outside staircase
and its landing.
Jesus looks and sighs.

The square is full of people around merchants of
foodstuffs, utensils, clothes and other items, all
either spread out on mats or in baskets on the
ground, with the merchants crouched in the
centre of their... shops or standing up, shouting
and gesticulating with stingy buyers.

'It's market day 'says Simon.

The main gate of the hotel where the Magi had stayed, is wide open and a line of donkeys laden with goods is coming out. Judas enters first and looks around haughtily and seizes a dirty hustler in short sleeves, with his short tunic reaching down to his knees. 'Hustler! 'he shouts. 'The landlord! Quick! Be quick. I am not used to being kept waiting for people. '

The boy runs away, dragging a broom behind him.
'But Judas! What manners! '
'Be quiet, Master. Leave me alone. It is important
that they consider us rich people coming from

town. '

The landlord rushes in, and bows down repeatedly before Judas, who looks impressive in Jesus' dark red mantle worn on top of his sumptuous yellow tunic full of fringes.

'We have come from far, man. We are Judaeans of the Asiatic communities. This gentleman, born in Bethlehem and persecuted, is now looking for some dear friends. We are with Him. We have come from Jerusalem, where we worshiped the Most High in His House. Can You give us some information? '

'My lord... your servant... will do everything for you. Give me your orders. '

'We want some information on many... and particularly on Anne, the woman whose house was opposite your hotel. '

'Oh! poor woman! You will find her only in Abraham's bosom. And her children with her. '

'Is she dead? How? '

'Don't you know of Herod's massacre? The whole world talked about it and even Caesar called him "a pig who feeds on blood". Oh! What have I said? Don't report me! Are you really Judaen? '

'Here is the sign of my tribe. So? Speak up. '

'Anne was killed by Herod's soldiers, with all her children, except one daughter. '

'But why? She was so good? '

'Did you know her? '

'Yes, very well. 'Judas lies brazen-faced.

'She was killed because she gave hospitality to those who said they were the father and mother of the Messiah... Come here, into this room... Walls have ears and it is dangerous to talk about certain things. '

They go into a low dark room and sit on a low couch.

'Now... I had a wonderful nose. I am not a hotel

keeper for nothing. I was born here, the son of sons of hotel keepers. Wiles are in my blood. And I did not take them. I could have found a hole for them. But... poor, unknown Galileans as they were... Oh! no! Hezekiah will not fall into the trap! And I felt... I felt they were different... that woman... Her eyes... something... no, no... She must have had a demon inside Her and She spoke to him. And She brought him... not to me... but to town. Anne was more innocent than a little lamb, and she gave them hospitality a few days later, when She already had the Child. They said He was the Messiah... Oh! the money I made during those days! The census was nothing like it! Many people came here who had nothing to do with the census. They came even from the seaside, even from Egypt to see... and it lasted for months! What a profit I made! The last to come were three kings, three powerful people, three magicians... I would not know! What a train! An endless one!

They took all the stables and they paid in gold for so much hay that could have lasted a month, and they went away the following day, leaving it all here. And what gifts they gave to the hustlers and the women!

And to me! Oh! I can only speak well of the Messiah, whether He was a true or false one. He made me earn bags of money. And I had no disasters. None of My family died, because I had just got married. So... but the others! '

'We would like to see the places of the slaughter. '

'The places? But every house was a place of slaughter. There were people killed for miles round Bethlehem. Come with me. '

They go up a staircase into a large terraced roof from where they can see a lot of the countryside and the whole of Bethlehem spread on the hills like an open fan.

'Can you see the ruined spots? Over there also the houses were burnt down because the fathers defended their children with their weapons. Can you see over there, that thing like a well-covered with ivy? Those are the remains of the synagogue. It was burnt down with the arch synagogue who declared that it was indeed the Messiah....burnt down by the survivors, driven wild because of the slaughter of their children. We had trouble for that after... And over there, and there, there... see those sepulchres? The victims are buried there.. They look like little sheep spread all over the green, as far as the eye can see. All the innocents and their fathers and mothers... See that vat? Its water was red after the killers washed their weapons and hands in it. And the brook at the back here, did you see it? It was pink with the blood, which had flowed into it from the sewers. And there, over there, in front of us. That is what is left of Anne's house.'

Jesus is crying.

'Did You know her well? '

Judas replies: 'She was like a sister for His Mother. Is that right, my friend? '

'Yes. ' says Jesus, simply.

'I understand ' remarks the hotel keeper who becomes pensive. Jesus bends forward to speak to Judas in a low voice.

'My friend would like to go on those ruins 'says Judas.

'Let Him go! They belong to everybody! '

They return downstairs, say goodbye and go out leaving the host who had been hoping to earn something, disappointed.

They cross the square and climb up the little staircase left standing over the ruins of Anne's house and onto the landing which is about two meters higher than the square. Jesus is standing against the little wall enclosing the landing, with nothing behind Him. From the square, His figure is clearly outlined against the sun shining behind Him, forming a halo around His golden hair and turning His snow white linen tunic- the only garment still on Him- a gleaming white. His mantle has slipped off His shoulders and now lies at His feet like a multi-coloured pedestal.

'From here 'says Jesus, 'My Mother made Me wave My hand to the Three Wise Men and we left from here to go to Egypt. '

People look at the four men on the ruins and one asks: 'Are they relatives of Anne? '

'They are friends. '

'Don't do any harm to the poor dead woman...' one woman shouts '...don't you do it, as her other friends did when she was alive, and then they ran away. '

Jesus is standing on the landing against the little wall enclosing it with nothing behind Him but the unkempt background of what was once Anne's kitchen garden and field now laid waste and strewn with debris. The outline of His figure is clearly cut against the sun shining behind Him: it forms a halo around His golden hair, and makes His snow white linen tunic look even whiter as it is the only garment on Him, since His mantle has slipped off His shoulders and is now lying at His feet like a multi-coloured pedestal.

Jesus stretches out His arms but when Judas sees the gesture he says: 'Don't speak! It isn't wise! '

But Jesus' powerful voice fills the square: 'Men of Judah! Men of Bethlehem, listen! Women of the land sacred to Rachel, listen! Listen to One Who descends from David, and having suffered from persecutions, has become worthy of speaking, and is speaking to you to give you light and comfort.

Listen. '
The people stop shouting, quarreling and buying and they gather together.
'He is a rabbi! '
'He certainly comes from Jerusalem. '
'Who is He? '
'What a handsome man! '
'And what a voice! '
'And His manners! '
'Of course, He is of David's House! '
'He is one of ours, then! '
'Let's listen to Him! '
The whole crowd is now gathered near the little staircase that looks like a pulpit.
'In Genesis it is said: "I will make you enemies of each other: you and the woman: She will crush your head and you will strike at Her heel." It is also said: "I will multiply your pains in childbearing... and the soil shall yield you brambles and thistles." That was the sentence against man, woman and the serpent. I have come from far to revere Rachel's tomb, and in the evening breeze, in the dew of the night, in the plaintive morning song of the nightingale,
 I heard ancient Rachel's sobs repeated, and they were repeated by the mouths of many mothers of Bethlehem, within their tombs or within their hearts. And I heard Jacob's sorrow roar in the pain of the widowed husbands deprived of their wives, whom sorrow had killed... I cry with you... But listen, brethren of My land. Bethlehem; the blessed land, the least of the towns in Judah, but the greatest in the eyes of God and of mankind, roused Satan's hatred because it was the cradle of the Saviour, as Micah says, destined to be the tabernacle on which the Glory of God, the Fire of God, His Incarnate Love was to rest.
"I will make you enemies of each other: you and

the woman; She will crush your head and you will strike at Her heel." Which enmity is there greater than the one that aims at a mother's children, the very heart of a woman? And which heel is there stronger than the Saviour's Mother's? The revenge of Satan defeated was therefore a natural one: he did not strike at the heel, but at the hearts of mothers, because of the Mother.
Oh! Pains were multiplied when the children were lost after having giving birth to them! Oh! great was the trouble of being a childless father after sowing and toiling for the offspring! And yet, Bethlehem, rejoice! Your pure blood, the blood of the innocents has prepared a blazing purple way for the Messiah... '
At the mention of the Saviour and the Mother, the crowd became increasingly turbulent and is now showing clear signs of agitation.
'Be quiet, Master and let us go 'says Judas.
But Jesus goes on: '... for the Messiah that the Grace of the God-Father saved from tyrants to preserve Him for His people and its salvation and... '
The shrill voice of a woman yelling hysterically cuts through'... 'Five, five I gave birth to, and not one is now in my house. Poor me! '
The uproar begins.
Another woman, rolls over in the dust, she tears her dress and shows a breast maimed of its nipple, shouting: 'Here, here on this mamma they slaughtered my first-born son! The sword cut off his face and my nipple at the same time. Oh! my Ellis! '
'And what about me! What about me? There is my royal palace. Three tombs in one, watched over by the father: my husband and children together. There, there! If there is a Saviour, let Him give me back my children, my husband, let Him save me

from despair, from Beelzebub He must save me. '
They all shout: 'Our children, our husbands, our
fathers! Let Him give them back, if He exists! '
Jesus waves His arms imposing silence. 'Brethren
of My land: I would like to give you back your
children, in their flesh. But I tell you: be good, be
resigned, forgive, hope, rejoice in hope and exult in
one certainty: you will soon have your children,
angels in Heaven, because the Messiah is about to
open the gates of Heaven, and if you are just,
death will be a new Life and a new Love... '
'Ah! Are You the Messiah? In the name of God, tell
us. '
Jesus lowers His arms in so sweet and kind a
gesture as though He were embracing them all,
and He says:
'Yes, I am. '
'Go away! Go away! It's Your fault, then! ' There are
hisses and jeers and a stone cuts through the air
heading for the landing.
Judas reacting instinctively, jumps in front of
Jesus, standing on the low wall of the landing,
with his mantle opened wide and undaunted, he
shields Jesus from the stones. The stone catches
Judas in the face, drawing blood but he shouts to
John and Simon: 'Take Jesus away. Behind those
trees. I'll follow. Go, in the name of Heaven! 'And
he shouts to the crowd: 'Mad dogs! I am of the
Temple and I will report you to the Temple and to
Rome. '
For a moment, the crowd is frightened. Then the
shower of stones resumes at once but fortunately,
their aim is off. And Judas, fearless, catches a
stone thrown at him and throws it back on the
head of an old man who is shouting like a magpie
being plucked alive! Judas also replies with
offensive language to the curses of the crowd.

22

When the crowd tries to climb up to his pedestal, he comes down from the little wall, quickly picks up an old branch from the ground, and mercilessly swings it round on backs, heads and hands. Some soldiers rush to the spot and with their lances they make their way through the crowd: 'Who are You? Why this brawl? '

'I am Judaean and I have been attacked by these plebeians. A rabbi, well known to the priests, was with me. He was speaking to these dogs. But they became wild and attacked us. '

'Who are You? '

'Judas of Kerioth, I was a man of the Temple. Now, I am a disciple of rabbi Jesus of Galilee and a friend of Simon the Pharisee, of Johanan the Sadducee, and of Joseph of Arimathaea, the Counsellor of the Sanhedrin, and finally, of Eleazar ben Anna, the Proconsul's great friend, and you can check. '

'I will. Where are you going? '

'I am going to Kerioth with my friend, then to Jerusalem. '

'Go. We will protect your back. '

Judas hands some coins to the soldier. It is illegal... but quite common, because the soldier takes them swiftly and cautiously, salutes and smiles. Judas jumps down from his platform and goes through the uncultivated field, skipping now and again until he reaches his companions.

'Are you seriously hurt? '

'No, it's nothing, Master! In any case, it's for You... But I gave them a licking as well. I must be covered with blood... '

'Yes, on your cheek. There is a rivulet here. '

John moistens a small piece of cloth and wipes Judas' cheek.

'I am sorry, Judas... But see... to tell them that we are Judaeans, according to your good practical sense... '

'They are beasts. I believe You are now convinced, Master. And I hope you will not insist... '

'Oh! no! Not because I am afraid. But because it is useless, just now. When they do not want us, we must not curse them, but withdraw praying for the poor, foolish people, who die of starvation and cannot see the Bread. Let us go along this out-of-the-way path, towards the shepherds, if we can find them. I think we will be able to get on to the toad to Hebron... '

'To have more stones thrown at us? '

'No. To say to them: "I am here." '

'What?... They will certainly beat us. They have been suffering for thirty years because of You. '

'We will see. '

And they disappear into a cool, shady, thick little wood.

Jesus And The Shepherds Elias, Levi And Joseph.

The hills rise higher and higher and the woods
grow thicker the further away from Bethlehem
until they form a real chain of mountain. Jesus,
climbing ahead, looks silently around as one
anxious to find something. He listens, more to the
voices of the woods than to the apostles' who are a
few yards behind Him and are speaking to one
another. Listening, He catches the ding-dong of a
bell carried in the wind and smiles. Then turning
round, He says;
'I hear the bells of sheep.'
'Where, Master?'
'I think near that hillock. But the wood prevents
Me from seeing.'
Because of the heat, the apostles have taken off
their mantles, rolled them up and are carrying
them across their backs. Without another word,
John also takes off his outer tunic and now, only
with his short inner tunic on, he throws his arms
around a tall smooth trunk of an ash tree and
climbs up....until he can see.
'Yes, Master. There are many herds and three
shepherds over there, behind that thicket.'
He comes back down and they proceed, sure of
their way.
'Will it be them? '
'We shall ask, Simon, and if they are not, they will

tell us something... They know one another. '

After about a hundred yards, they emerge onto a
wide green pasture fully surrounded by gigantic
very old trees and many sheep grazing on the thick
grass of the undulating meadow. There are also
three men, watching over the sheep: One old with
hair all turned white, a second man of about
thirty and the third of about forty years of age.
'Be careful, Master. They are herdsmen... 'cautions
Judas, when he sees Jesus hastening His step.
But, without responding to Judas, Jesus hurries
on, tall and handsome in His white tunic and with
the setting sun in front of Him, He seems bright as
an angel...

'Peace be with you, My friends 'He greets when He reaches the edge of the meadow.
The three men turn round, surprised. There is a silent pause....and then the eldest man asks:

'Who are You? '
'One Who loves you. '
'You would be the first in so many years. Where are You from? '
'From Galilee. '
'From Galilee? Oh! ' The man watches Him carefully....and the other two draw nearer.
'From Galilee ' repeats the shepherd. And in a very low voice, as one speaking to himself, he adds 'He came from Galilee, too' aloud again, the shepherd asks again 'From which town, my Lord? '
'From Nazareth. '
'Oh! Well, tell me. Has a Child ever come back to Nazareth, a Child with a woman whose name was Mary and a man called Joseph, a Child, Who was even more beautiful than His Mother, so beautiful that I have never seen a fairer flower on the slopes of Judah? A Child born in Bethlehem of Judah, at the time of the edict? A Child Who later fled, most fortunately for the world. A Child, oh! I would give my life just to hear whether He is alive... He must be a man by now. '
'Why do you say that His flight was a great fortune for the world? '
'Because He was the Saviour, the Messiah and Herod wanted Him dead. I was not there when He fled with His father and Mother. When I heard of the slaughter and I came back... because also I had children (he sobs), my Lord, and a wife... (he sobs), and I heard they had been killed (he sobs again), but I swear by the God of Abraham, I was more afraid for Him than for my own family – I heard He had fled and I could not even enquire; I could not even take away my own slaughtered creatures... They threw stones at me, as they do with lepers and unclean people, they treated me like a murderer... and I had to hide in the woods, and live like a wolf... until I found a master. Oh!

28

it's no longer Anne... He is hard and cruel... If a sheep gets hurt, if a wolf preys on a lamb, he either beats me till I bleed or he takes my poor pay, and I have to work in the woods for other people, I must do something, to pay him back three times the value.

But it does not matter. I have always said to the Most High: "Let me see Your Messiah, at least let me know that He is alive, and all the rest is nothing." My Lord, I have told You how the people in Bethlehem treated me, and how my master deals with me. I could have repaid them in their own coins, I could have wronged them, stealing, so that I would not suffer under my master. But I preferred to suffer, to forgive, to be honest, because the angels said: "Glory to God in the Highest Heaven and peace on earth to men of good will." '

'Is that what they said? '

'Yes, they did, my Lord, You must believe, at least You, Who are good. You must know and believe that the Messiah is born. No one would believe it any longer. But angels do not lie... and we were not drunk, as they said. This man here, was a boy then, and he was the first to see the angel. He drank but milk. Can milk make one drunk? The angels said: "Today, in the town of David the Saviour was born, He is Christ, the Lord. And here is a sign for you. You will find a Child wrapped in swaddling clothes lying in a manger." '

'Did they say exactly that? Did you not misunderstand them? Are you not mistaken, after such a long time? '

'Oh! no! Isn't it, Levi? In order not to forget, – we could not forget in any case, because they were heavenly words and were written in our hearts with a heavenly fire – every morning, every evening, when the sun rises, when the first star

starts shining, we repeat them as a prayer, as a
blessing, to have strength and comfort in His name
and in His Mother's. '
'Ah! You said: "Christ"? '
'No, my Lord. We say: "Glory to God in the Highest
Heaven and peace on earth to men of good will,
through Jesus Christ Who was born of Mary in a
stable in Bethlehem and Who, wrapped in
swaddling clothes, was in a manger, He Who is the
Saviour of the world." '
'But, in short, whom are you looking for? '
'Jesus Christ, the Son of Mary, the Nazarene, the
Saviour. '
'It is I. ' And Jesus is radiant as He reveals Himself
to His persevering, faithful and patient lovers.
'You! Oh! Lord, Saviour, Our Jesus!' The three men
prostrate themselves on the ground and kiss
Jesus' feet, crying with joy.
'Stand up. Get up. Elias and you, Levi and you,
whose name I do not know. '
'Joseph, the son of Joseph. '
'These are My disciples, John, a Galilean, Simon
and Judas, Judaeans. '
The shepherds are no longer prostrated on the
ground, but kneeling, sitting back on their heels.
And thus, they worship the Saviour with loving
eyes and trembling lips, whilst their faces blanch
and blush with joy. Jesus sits down on the grass.
'No, my Lord. You, King of Israel, must not sit on
the grass. '
'Never mind, My dear friends. I am poor. A
carpenter as far as the world is concerned. I am
rich only in My love for the world, and in the love I
get from good people. I have come to stay with you,
to share the evening meal with you and sleep
beside you on the hay, and to be comforted by
you... '
'Oh! comfort! We are coarse and persecuted. '

'I am persecuted, too. But you give Me what I seek: love, faith and hope, a hope that will last for years and bear flowers. See? You waited for Me and you believed without the least doubt, that I was the Messiah. And I have come to you. '

'Oh! Yes! You have come. Now, even if I die, I will not be upset that I hoped in vain. '

'No, Elias. You will live until Christ's triumph and after. You saw My dawn, you must see My glory. And what about the others? You were twelve: Elias, Levi, Samuel, Jonah, Isaac, Tobias, Jonathan, Daniel, Simeon, John, Joseph, Benjamin. My Mother always mentioned your names to Me. Because you were My first friends. '

'Oh! ' The shepherds are more and more moved. 'Where are the others? '

'Old Samuel died of old age about twenty years ago. Joseph was killed because he fought at the gate of the enclosure to give time to his wife who had just become a mother a few hours before, to escape with this man, whom I took with me for the sake of my friend... also to have children around me once again. I took Levi also with me... He was persecuted. Benjamin is a shepherd on Lebanon with Daniel. Simeon, John and Tobias, who now wants to be called Matthew in memory of his father who was also killed, are disciples of John. Jonah works on the plain of Esdraelon for a Pharisee. Isaac suffers very much from his back which is bent in two. He lives in dire poverty, all by himself at Juttah. We help him as much as we can, but we have all been badly hit and our help is like dew drops on a fire. Jonathan is now the servant of one of Herod's big men. '

'How did you, and particularly Jonathan, Jonah, Daniel and Benjamin get such jobs? '

'I remembered Your relative Zacharias... Your Mother had sent me to him. When we were in the mountain gorges in Judaea, fugitives and cursed, I took them to him. He was good to us. He sheltered and fed us. And he found work for us. He did what he could. I had already taken all Anne's herd for the Herodian... and I remained with him... When the Baptist, grown into a man, began to preach, Simeon, John and Tobias went to him. '

'But now the Baptist is in jail. '

'Yes, and they are keeping watch near Machaerus, with a few sheep, to avoid arousing suspicion. They were given the sheep by a rich man, a disciple of Your relative John. '

'I would like to see them all. '

'Yes, My Lord. We will go and say to them: "Come, He is alive. He remembers us and loves us." '

'And He wants you to be His friends. '

'Yes, my Lord. '

'But we will go first to Isaac. And where are Samuel and Joseph buried? '

'Samuel in Hebron. He remained in Zacharias' service. Joseph... has no tomb. He was burned with the house. '

'He is no longer in the cruel fire, but in the flames of God's love and will soon be in His glory. I am telling you, and particularly you, Joseph, son of Joseph. Come here, that I may kiss you to thank your father. '

'And my children? '

'They are angels, Elias. Angels who will repeat the "Gloria" when the Saviour is crowned. '

'King? '

'No, Redeemer. Oh! What a procession of just people and saints! And in front there will be the white and purple phalanges of the martyrs! As soon as the gates of Limbo are opened, we shall ascend together to the eternal Kingdom. And then you will come and will find your fathers, mothers and children in the Lord! Believe Me. '

'Yes, my Lord. '

'Call Me: Master. It is getting dark, the first evening star is beginning to shine. Say your prayer before supper. '

'Not I. You say it, please. '

The disciples and shepherds remain kneeling whilst Jesus stands up and with His arms outstretched, He prays:

'Glory to God in the highest Heaven, and peace on earth to men of good will who have deserved to see the Light and serve it. The Saviour is among them. The Shepherd of the royal line is with His herd. The morning Star has risen. Rejoice, just people! Rejoice in the Lord. He Who made the vaults of heaven and has strewn them with stars, Who placed the seas at the boundaries of the land, Who created winds and dew, and fixed the course of seasons to give bread and wine to His children, He now sends you a more Sublime food: the living Bread that descends from Heaven, the Wine of the eternal Vine. Come to Me, you who are the first of My worshippers. Come to meet the Eternal Father in truth, to follow Him in holiness and receive His eternal reward. '

The shepherds offer bread and new milk, and as there are only three emptied marrows used for bowls, Jesus is the first to eat, with Simon and Judas. Then John, to whom Jesus hands His cup, with Levi and Joseph. Elias is last.

The sheep have stopped grazing and are now gathered together in a compact group perhaps waiting to be led to their enclosure. The three shepherds lead the sheep into the wood, to a rustic shed made with branches and enclosed by ropes. Then busily, make beds of hay for Jesus and His disciples, after which they light fires to keep wild animals away.

Judas and John lie down and tired as they are, they are soon fast asleep. Simon would like to keep Jesus company he too soon falls asleep shortly afterwards, sitting on the hay and leaning against a pole.
 Jesus remains awake with the shepherds and they talk about Joseph, Mary, the flight into Egypt, their return... and after such questions about loving friendship, the shepherds ask more noble questions like what they can do to serve Jesus? How will they, poor, rough shepherds, be able to do anything?

And Jesus teaches them and then explains: 'Now I am going to go through Judaea. My disciples will keep in touch with you all the time. Later I will let you come. In the meantime, get together. Make sure that you are all in touch with one another and that everyone knows that I am here, in this world, as Master and Saviour. Let everybody know, as best as you can. I will not promise that you will be believed. I have been mocked at and beaten. They will do the same to you.
But as you have been strong and just in your long expectation, persist in being so, now that you are Mine. Tomorrow, we will go towards Juttah. Then to Hebron. Can you come? '
'Of course, we can. The roads belong to everybody and the pastures to God. Only Bethlehem is forbidden by an unfair hatred. The other villages know... but they jeer at us, calling us "topers". Thus we will not be able to do very much here. '
 'I will employ you elsewhere. I will not abandon you. '
'For all our lifetimes? '

'For all My lifetime. '

'No, Master, I will die first. I am old. '

'Do you think so? I do not. One of the first faces I saw, Elias, was yours. It will also be one of the last. I will take with Me, impressed in My eyes, the image of your face deranged by sorrow for My death. But after, you will treasure in your heart the memory of the joy of a triumphal morning and will thus await death... Death: the everlasting meeting with Jesus, Whom you adored when He was a baby. Also then the angels will sing the Gloria: "for the man of good will." '

Jesus At Juttah With The Shepherd Isaac.

It is early morning and the silvery tinkling of a little torrent fills the valley as its foamy waters flow southwards among the rocks, spreading its gay freshness out onto the little pastures along its banks but its moisture seems to climb up to the very green slopes of the hills, from the soil right through the bushes and shrubs of the brushwood and reaching right up to the top of the tall trees of the wood, mostly walnuts, giving the slope their beautiful varied shades of emerald green. Here and there in the wood are many green open spaces covered with thick grass that makes good healthy pasture for herds.

Jesus is walking down towards the torrent with His disciples and the three shepherds and now and again, He stops patiently to wait for a sheep that has been left behind or a shepherd who has had to run after a lamb that has gone astray- the Good Shepherd, He has provided Himself with a long branch to clear His path from blackberry, hawthorn and clematis branches that stick out in all directions and catch on garments, and the stick completes His pastoral figure.

'See? Juttah is up there. We will cross the torrent; there is a ford, which is very useful in summer, without having to use the bridge. It would have been quicker to come via Hebron. But You did not want that. '

'No. We will go to Hebron later. We must always go first to those who suffer. The dead do not suffer any longer when they have been just people. And Samuel was a just man. And if the dead need our prayers, it is not necessary to be near their bones to pray for them.

Bones? What are they? A proof of the power of God Who made man with dust. Nothing else.

Also animals have bones. But the skeletons of all animals are not so perfect as a man's skeleton. Only man, the king of creation, has an upright position, as a king over his subjects, and his face looks forwards and upwards without having to twist his neck; man looks upwards, towards the Abode of the Father. But they are still bones. Dust which will return to dust. The eternal Bounty has decided to assemble them again on the eternal Day to give an even greater joy to the blessed souls. Just imagine: not only the souls will be reunited and will love one another as and even more than they did on the earth, but they will rejoice also seeing one another with the same features they had on the earth: dear curly-haired children, like yours, Elias, fathers and mothers with loving hearts and faces like yours Levi and Joseph. Nay, in your case Joseph, it will be the day when at last you will see the faces for which you feel nostalgia. There are no more orphans, no widows among the just, up there...

Prayers for the dead can be said anywhere. It is the prayer of a soul for the soul of a relative to the Perfect Spirit, Who is God, Who is everywhere. Oh! holy freedom of what is spiritual! There are no distances, no exile, no prisons, no tombs... There is nothing that can divide or restrict in painful impotence what is outside and above the chains of the flesh. You will go with your better part, towards your beloved ones. And they will come to you with their better part.

And the whole effusion of loving souls will rotate around the Eternal Fulcrum, around God: the Most Perfect Spirit, the Creator of everything that was, is and will be, Love that loves you and teaches you how to love... But here we are at the ford. I can see a row of stones emerging from the shallow water. '

'Yes, Master, it is that one there. At the time of floods, it is a roaring waterfall. Now there are seven streamlets flowing placidly between the six large stones of the ford. '

They reach the crossing where six large square-cut stones are laid about a foot apart from each other, across the torrent and the water, which reaches the stones in one large sparkling ribbon, is divided into seven minor ones that rush happily to re-join together again beyond the ford, to once again form one fresh stream that flows, babbling among the stones.

The shepherds watch the sheep cross, some walking on the stones, others preferring to cross in the stream that is only a foot deep and they drink the pure gurgling water.

Jesus crosses on the stones followed by His disciples and they resume walking on the other bank.

'You told me that You want to inform Isaac that You are here, but You do not want to go into the village? '

'Yes, that is what I want. '

'Well, we had better part. I will go to him, Levi and Joseph will stay with the herd and with You. I'll go up here. It will be quicker. '

And Elias starts to climb up the mountain side, towards the white houses that are so bright up there in the sunshine.

He reaches the first houses and goes along a tiny path between houses and kitchen gardens and walks thus for about ten meters and then turns into a wider road and entering into the square. The morning market is still on the square and housewives and vendors are shouting under the shady trees of the square.

Without stopping, Elias moves resolutely to the end of the square and an attractive street begins, to a little house, or rather, a room with the door wide open. Almost on its threshold, in a little bed, lies an emaciated sick man asking passers-by for alms in a plaintive voice. Elias dashes in.

'Isaac... it's me. '

'You? I was not expecting you. You were here last month. '

'Isaac... Isaac... Do you know why I have come? '

'No, I don't... You are excited. What's happening? '

'I have seen Jesus of Nazareth, He is a man, now, a rabbi. He came looking for me... and He wants to see us. Oh! Isaac! Are you not well? '

Isaac, in fact, has fallen back as if he were dying. But he comes round: 'No. The news... Where is He? What is He like? Oh! If I could see Him! '

'He is down in the valley. He sent me to say to you exactly this: "Come, Isaac, because I want to see you and bless you." I'll call someone now to help me and I'll take you down. '

'Is that what He said? '

'Yes, it is. But what are you doing? '

'I'm going. '

Isaac throws away the blankets, he moves his paralyzed legs, he throws them off the straw mattress, he puts his feet on the floor, he stands up, still somewhat hesitating, and shaky. It all happens in an instant, under Elias' wide open eyes... who at last understands and begins to shout...

A little woman looks in curiously. She sees the sick man stand up and cover himself with one of the blankets, since he has nothing else, and run away, shouting like a mad man.

'Let us go... this way, it will be quicker and we will not meet the crowd... Quick, Elias. 'They run through a little door of a kitchen garden in the back, they push the gate, made of dry branches, and once outside, they run along a narrow dirty path, then down a little road along kitchen gardens and finally through meadows and thickets, right down to the torrent.

'There is Jesus, over there 'says Elias, pointing Him out. 'The tall, handsome one, with fair hair, with a white tunic and red mantle... '

Isaac runs, he cuts through the grazing sheep, and with a cry of triumph, joy and adoration he prostrates himself at Jesus' feet.

'Stand up, Isaac. I have come. To bring you peace and blessings. Stand up, that I may see your face. '

But Isaac cannot stand up, overcome with excitement as he is and he remains prostrated, with his face on the ground, crying happily.

'You came at once. You did not worry whether you could... '

'You told me to come... and I came. '

'He did not even close the door or pick up the alms, Master. '

'It does not matter. The angels will watch his house. Are you happy, Isaac? '

'Oh! My Lord! '

'Call Me Master. '

'Yes, my Lord, my Master. Even if you had not cured me, I would have been happy to see You. How could I find so much grace with You? '

'Because of your faith and patience, Isaac. I know
how much you suffered... '
'Nothing! nothing! It does not matter! I have found
You. You are alive. You are here. That's what
matters. The rest, all the rest is over. But, my Lord
and my Master, You are not going away any more,
is that right? '
'Isaac, I have the whole of Israel to evangelize. I am
going... But if I cannot stay, you can always serve
and follow Me. Do you want to be My disciple,
Isaac? '
'Oh! But I am not capable! '
'Can you avow Who I am? Avow it against jeers and
threats? And tell people that I called you and you
came? '
'Even if You did not want, I would avow all that. I
would disobey You in that, Master. Forgive me for
saying so. '
Jesus smiles. 'You can see then that you are
capable of becoming a disciple! '
'Oh! If that's all one has to do! I thought it was
more difficult, that we had to go to school with the
rabbis to learn how to serve You, the Rabbi of
rabbis... and to go to school at my age... 'The man
in fact must be at least fifty years old.
'You have done your schooling already, Isaac. '
'Me? No. '
'Yes, you have. Have you not continued to believe
and love, to respect and bless God and your
neighbour, not to be envious, not to wish what
belongs to other people, and even what was your
own and you no longer possessed, to speak only
the truth, even if it should be harmful to you, not
to associate with Satan committing sins? Have you
not done all these things, in the last thirty years of
misfortunes? '
'Yes, Master. '
'So you see, you have done your schooling. Go on

doing so and, in addition, reveal to the world that I am in the world. There is nothing else to be done. '

'I have already preached You, Lord Jesus. I preached You to the children, who used to come, when I arrived lame in this village, begging for bread and doing some work, such as shearing and dairy work, and the children used to come round my bed, when I got worse and I was paralyzed from my waist downwards. I spoke of You to the children of many years ago, and to the children of present times, who are the sons of the previous ones... Children are good and they always believe... I told them of Your birth... of the angels... of the Star and the Wise Men... and of Your Mother... Oh! Tell me! Is She alive?'

'She is alive and She sends you Her regards. She always spoke of you all. '

'Oh! If I could see Her! '

'You will see Her. You will come to My house one day. Mary will greet you saying: "My friend". '

'Mary... yes, when you utter that name it is like filling your mouth with honey... There is a woman in Juttah, she is a woman now, she had her fourth child not long ago, but once she was a little girl, one of my little friends... and she called her children: Mary and Joseph the first two, and as she dared not call the third one Jesus, she called him Immanuel, as a good omen for herself, her home and Israel. And she is now thinking of a name to give to her fourth child, born six days ago. Oh! When she hears that I am cured! And that You are here! Sarah is as good as homemade bread, and her husband Joachim is also so good. And their relatives? I owe them my life. They have always helped and sheltered me. '

'Let us go and ask them for hospitality during the hottest hours of the day and to bless them for their charity. '

'This way, Master. It is easier for the sheep and we will avoid the people, who are most certainly excited. The old woman, who saw me getting up, will have certainly told them. '

They follow the torrent, departing from it further south, to take a steep path along the mountainside shaped like the prow of a ship, moving in the opposite direction to the torrent now running along a beautiful uneven valley formed by the intersection of two mountain ranges.

A little dry-stone wall marks the boundaries of the estate that declines towards the valley. On the meadow, there are apple, fig and walnut trees, a kitchen garden with a well, the pergola and the flower beds and further along, a white house surrounded by green lawns, with a protruding wing that protects the staircase and forms a porch and loggia with a little dome on the highest part. There is a lot of shouting coming from the house. Walking ahead, Isaac goes in and calls at the top of his voice: 'Mary, Joseph, Immanuel! Where are you? Come to Jesus. '

Three little ones: a girl of about five years old, and two little boys, about four and two years of age, run to Isaac, the youngest still somewhat uncertain on his legs. They are dumbfounded to see the... revived man. Then the little girl shouts: 'Isaac! Mummy! Isaac is here! Judith was right. '

A tall, buxom, brown, lovely woman emerges from a noisy room, most beautiful in her best dress: a snow-white linen dress, like a rich chemise falling in puckers down to her ankles. It is tied at her shapely waist with a multi-coloured striped shawl that covers her wonderful hips dropping in fringes down to her knees at the back. At the front, the chemise is tied under the filigree buckle and its ends hang loose.

A light veil decorated with rose branches on a beige background is pinned to her black plaits, like a tiny turban, and falls on to her neck in flowing folds and then onto her shoulders and breasts. It is held tight on her head by a small crown of medals tied together by a little chain. Heavy rings hang from her ears, and her tunic is held close to her neck by a silver necklace that passes through eyelets of her dress. And there are heavy silver bracelets on her arms.

'Isaac! What's this? Judith... I thought she had gone mad... But you are walking! What happened? '

'The Saviour! Oh! Sarah! He is here! He has come! '

'Who? Jesus of Nazareth? Where is He? '

'Over there! Behind the walnut-tree, and He wishes to know if you will receive Him! '

'Joachim! Mother! Come here, all of you! The Messiah is here! '

Women, men, boys, little ones run out shouting and yelling... but when they see Jesus, tall and stately, they lose heart and become petrified.

'Peace to this house and to you all. The peace and blessing of God. 'Jesus walks slowly, smiling, towards the group. 'My friends: will you give hospitality to the Wayfarer? 'and He smiles even more. His smile overcomes all fears. The husband takes heart: 'Come in, Messiah. We have loved You before meeting You. We shall love You more after meeting You. The house is celebrating today for three reasons: for You, for Isaac and for the circumcision of my third son. Bless him, Master. Woman, bring the baby! Come in, my Lord. '

They go into a room decorated for the feast. There are tables with foodstuffs, carpets and branches everywhere.

Sarah comes back with a lovely new-born baby in

her arms and presents him to Jesus.

'May God be always with him. What is his name? '

'No name yet. This is Mary, this is Joseph, this is Immanuel... but this one has no name yet... 'Jesus looks at the parents, who are close to each other, He smiles: 'Find a name, if he is to be circumcised today... 'They look at each other, they look at Him, they open their mouths and close them again without saying anything. Everyone is paying attention.

Jesus insists: 'The history of Israel has so many great, sweet, blessed names. The sweetest and most blessed ones have already been given. But perhaps there are still some left. '

The parents cry out together: 'Yours, Lord! 'and the mother adds: 'But it is too holy... '

Jesus smiles and asks: 'When will he be circumcised? '

'We are waiting for the circumciser. '

'I will be present at the ceremony. And in the meantime I wish to thank you for what you have done for My Isaac. He no longer needs the help of good people. But good people still need God. You called your third son: God be with us. But you had God with you ever since you were charitable to My servant. May you be blessed. Your charity will be remembered in Heaven and on the earth. '

'Is Isaac going away now? Is he leaving us? '

'Does that upset you? But he must serve his Master. But he will come, and so will I. In the meantime, you will speak of the Messiah... There is so much to be said to convince the world! But here is the person you are expecting. '

A pompous personage comes in with a servant. There are greetings and low bows. 'Where is the child? 'he asks haughtily

'He is here. But greet the Messiah. He is here. '

'The Messiah! The one who cured Isaac? I heard

about it. But.. We will talk about it after. I am in a great hurry. The child and his name. '

The people present are mortified by the man's manners. But Jesus smiles as if the impoliteness was not addressed to Him. He takes the baby, He touches his little forehead with His beautiful fingers, as if He wanted to consecrate him and says: 'His name is Jesai ' and then hands him back to his father, who goes into another room with the haughty man and other people. Jesus stays where He is until they return with the child, who is screaming desperately.

'Woman, give Me the child. He will not cry any longer ' He says to comfort the distressed mother. In fact, the child, once he is laid on Jesus' knees, becomes silent.

Jesus forms a group of His own, with the little ones around Him, and also the shepherds and disciples. The sheep that Elias has put in an enclosure are bleating outside. There is the noise of a party in the house. They bring sweets and drinks to Jesus. But Jesus hands them out to the little ones.

'Are You not drinking, Master? Will You not have anything. We are offering it warmly. '

'I know, Joachim, and I accept wholeheartedly. But let Me make the little ones happy first. They are My joy... '

'Pay no attention to that man, Master. '

'No, Isaac. I will pray that he may see the Light. John, take the two little boys to see the sheep. And you, Mary, come closer to Me and tell Me: Who am I? '

'You are Jesus, the Son of Mary of Nazareth, born in Bethlehem. Isaac saw You and he gave me the name of Your Mother, that I may be good. '

'To imitate Her, you must be as good as an angel of God, purer than a lily that blooms on top of a mountain, as pious as the holiest Levite. Will you be like that? '

'Yes, Jesus, I will. '

'Say: Master or Lord, little girl. '

'Let her call Me with My name, Judas. Only when it is uttered by innocent lips, it does not lose the sound that it has on My Mother's lips.

Everybody, throughout future centuries, will mention that name, some because of an interest or other, some to curse it. Only innocent people, without any interest and any hatred, will pronounce it with the same love as this little girl and My Mother.

Also sinners will invoke Me, because they need mercy. But My Mother and the little ones! Why do you call Me Jesus? ' He asks, caressing the little girl.

'Because I love You... as I love my father, mother and my little brothers ' she replies, embracing Jesus' knees, and smiling with her head turned upwards. And Jesus bends down and kisses her.

Jesus At Hebron. Zacharias' House. Aglae.

'At what time will we be arriving?' asks Jesus,
walking at the centre of the group behind the
sheep, grazing on the grass on the banks.
'At about the third hour. It's almost ten miles '
replies Elias.
'Are we going to Kerioth afterwards?' asks Judas.
'Yes, we will go there.'
'Was it not quicker to go to Kerioth from Juttah? It
cannot be a great distance. Is that correct,
shepherd? '
'About two miles longer, more or less.'
'This way, we will be doing over twenty for nothing.'
'Judas, why are you so worried? '
'I am not worried, Master. But You promised You
would come to my house.'
'And I will. I always keep My promises.'
'I sent word to my mother... and after all, You said
so Yourself, one can be near the dead also with
one's soul.'
'I did. But just think, Judas: you have not yet
suffered because of Me. These people have been
suffering for thirty years, and they have never
betrayed, not even My memory. They did not know
whether I was dead or alive... and yet they
remained faithful. They remembered Me as a
newly-born baby, an infant with nothing but tears
and the need of milk... and they have always

worshipped Me as God. Because of Me they have
been beaten, cursed and persecuted as if they were
the disgrace of Judaea, and yet their faith has
never faltered. Neither did it wither under blows,
on the contrary it took deeper roots and became
stronger.‘

'By the way. For some days I have been anxious to
ask You a question. These people are Your friends
and the friends of God, are they not? The angels
blessed them with the peace of Heaven, did they
not? They have been faithful against all
temptations, have they not? Would You explain to
me, then, why they are unhappy? And what about
Anne? She was killed because she loved You…‘

'Are you therefore deducing that to be loved by Me
and to love Me brings bad luck?‘

'No... but...'
'But you are. I am sorry to see you so closed to the
Light and so open to human things. No, never
mind John, and you too, Simon. I prefer him to

speak. I never reproach. I only want you to open your souls to Me that I may enlighten them.

Come here, Judas, listen. You are basing yourself on an opinion that is common to many people of our times and will be common to many in future. I said: an opinion. I should say: an error. But since you do not do so out of malice, but out of ignorance of the truth, it is not an error, it is only an incorrect opinion like a child's. And you are like children, My poor men. And I am here, as a Master, to make adults of you, capable of telling the truth from the false, good from bad and what is better from what is good. Listen to Me, therefore. What is life? It is a period of pause, I would say the limbo of Limbo, that the God Father grants you as trial to ascertain whether you are good or bad children, after which He will allot, according to your deeds, a future life without pauses or trials. Now tell Me: would it be fair if a man, simply because he has been granted the rare gift of being in the position of serving God in a special way, had also an everlasting wealth throughout his life? Do you not think that he has already been granted a great deal and may therefore consider himself happy, even if human things are against him? Would it not be unfair if he, who already has the light of divine revelation in his heart and the smile of a clear conscience, should also have worldly honours and wealth? And would it not also be unwise?'

'Master, I would also say that he would be a desecrator. Why put human joys where You already are? When one has You – and they had You, they are the only rich people in Israel because they have had You for thirty years – one should have nothing else. We do not put human things on the Propitiatory... and the consecrated vase is used only for sacred uses. And these people are

consecrated since the day they saw Your smile...
and nothing but You is to enter their hearts,
which possess You. I wish I was like them! ' says
Simon.
'But you wasted no time, immediately after you
saw the Master and were cured, in getting back
your property ' Judas replies sarcastically.
'That is true. I said I would and I did. But do you
know why? How can you judge if you do not know
the whole situation? My representative was given
precise instructions. Now that Simon Zealot has
been cured – and his enemies can no longer harm
him, neither can they persecute him because he
belongs only to Jesus and to no sect: he has Jesus
and nothing else – Simon can dispose of his wealth
which an honest and faithful servant kept for him.
And I, being the owner for a further short time,
gave instructions that the estate should be
reorganised, so that I would get more money when
selling it and I would be able to say... no, I am not
telling what.'
'The angels tell, Simon and they are writing it in
the eternal book ' says Jesus.
Simon looks at Jesus. Their eyes meet: Simon's
express surprise, Jesus' blessing approval.
'As usual. I am wrong.'
'No, Judas. You have a practical sense, you said so
yourself. '
'Oh! but with Jesus!... Also Simon Peter was full of
practical sense, now instead!... You, too, Judas,
will become like him. You have only been with the
Master a short time, we have been longer with Him
and we are already better ' says John who is
always kind and conciliatory.
'He did not want me. Otherwise I would have been
His since Passover. ' says Judas plaintively.
Jesus puts an end to the argument by asking Levi:
'Have you ever been to Galilee? '

'Yes, my Lord. '

'You will come with Me to take Me to Jonah. Do you know him? '

'Yes, I do. We always met at Passover. I used to go and see him then.'

Joseph, mortified, lowers his head. Jesus notices and says: 'You cannot both come. Elias would be left alone with the sheep. But you will come with Me as far as the Jericho pass where we will part for some time. I will tell you afterwards what you have to do. '

'What about us? Will we not do anything? '

'Yes, you will, Judas, you will.'

'There are some houses over there ' says John, walking a few steps in front of the others.

'It's Hebron. Between two rivers with its crest. See, Master? That house there, amidst all the green, a little higher up than the others? That's Zacharias' house.'

'Let us quicken our paces.'

The sheep's little hooves click like castanets on the uneven stones of the roughly paved road as they quicken their pace, rapidly cover the last stretch of the road and enter the village.

People stare at the group of men, so different by look, age and garments amongst the white sheep. They reach the house.

'Oh! It's different! There was a gate here! ' says Elias. Now, instead, there is a metal door that prevents one from seeing, and also the enclosure wall is higher than a man and thus nothing can be seen inside.

'Perhaps it will be open at the back. 'They go round a large rectangular wall but find it is the same height all round.

'The wall was built not long ago ' remarks John, examining it. 'There is not a scratch on it and there is still lime rubble on the ground. '

'I cannot even see the sepulchre... It was near the wood. Now the wood is outside the wall and... and it seems to belong to everybody. They are gathering firewood in it. 'Elias is puzzled.

A small but strong looking man, an old woodcutter, who is watching the group, stops sawing a trunk lying on the ground and goes towards the group. 'Whom are you looking for?'

'We wanted to go in to pray on Zacharias' tomb '.

'There is no tomb any longer. Don't you know? Who are you? '

'I am a friend of Samuel, the shepherd. This... '

'It is not necessary, Elias ' says Jesus and Elias keeps quiet.

'Ah! Samuel!... I see! But since John, Zacharias' son, was put into prison, the house is no longer his. And it is a misfortune because all the profit of his property was given to the poor people in Hebron. One morning a man came from Herod's court, he threw Jowehel out, he affixed seals, then he came back with bricklayers and they started raising the wall... The sepulchre was over there in the corner. He did not want it... and one morning we found it all spoiled and half destroyed... the poor bones all scattered... We put them together again as well as we could... They are now in a sarcophagus... And in the house of the priest, Zacharias, that filthy man keeps his lovers. Now there is a mime from Rome. That is why he raised the wall. He does not want people to see... The house of the priest a brothel! The house of the miracle and of the Precursor! For it is certainly him, if he is not the Messiah. And how much trouble we had because of the Baptist! But he is our great man! He is really great! Even when he was born there was a miracle. Elizabeth was as old as a withered thistle but she became as fruitful as an apple in Adar* and that was the first miracle.

Then a cousin of hers came and She was a holy woman and She served her and loosened the priest's tongue. Her name was Mary. I remember Her although we saw Her very rarely. How it happened I don't know. They say that to make Elizabeth happy, She made Zacharias put his mute mouth against Her pregnant bosom or that She put Her fingers into his mouth. I don't know. It is a fact that after nine months' silence, Zacharias spoke praising the Lord and saying that there was a Messiah. He did not explain more. But my wife was there that day and she assured me that Zacharias, praising the Lord, said that his son would precede Him. Now I say: it is not what people believe. John is the Messiah and he goes before the Lord, as Abraham went before God. That's what it is. Am I not right? '

*Adar is the sixth month in the Jewish calendar falling between February and March.

'You are right with regard to the spirit of the Baptist, who always proceeds before God. But you are not right with regard to the Messiah'
'Well, the woman who said that She was the Mother of the Son of God – Samuel said so – was it not true that She was? Is She still living? '
'Yes, She was. The Messiah was born, preceded by him who raised his voice in the desert, as the Prophet said.'
'You are the first to say so. John, the last time that Jowehel took him a sheepskin, which he did every year at the beginning of winter, although he was questioned about the Messiah, did not say: "The Messiah is here." When he will say so...'
'Man, I was a disciple of John and I heard him say: "Here is the Lamb of God" pointing to... ' says John.

56

'No, no. He is the Lamb. A true Lamb who grew up by himself, almost without the need of a father and mother. As soon as he became a son of the Law, he lived isolated in the mountain caves overlooking the desert, and he grew up there conversing with God. Elizabeth and Zacharias died, and he did not come. God only was his father and mother. There is no holy man greater than he is. You can ask everyone in Hebron. Samuel used to say so, but the people in Bethlehem must have been right. John is the holy man of God. '

'If someone said to you: "I am the Messiah", what would you say? ' asks Jesus.

'I would call him a "blasphemer" and I would drive him away, throwing stones at him. '

'And if he worked a miracle to prove that he was the Messiah? '

'I would say that he was "possessed". The Messiah will come when John reveals himself in his true nature. The very hatred of Herod is the proof. Cunning as he is, he knows that John is the Messiah.'

'He was not born in Bethlehem.'

'But when he is freed, after announcing by himself his impending coming, he will reveal himself in Bethlehem. Also Bethlehem is waiting for that. Whilst... Oh! Go, if you have plenty of guts, and talk to the Bethlehemites of another Messiah... and you will see...'

'Have you a synagogue?'

'Yes, about two hundred steps straight ahead. You cannot go wrong. Near it there is the sarcophagus with the violated remains.'

'Goodbye, may God enlighten you.'

They go away, make a right turn on to the front of the house and find, at its door, a beautiful young impudently dressed woman. 'My Lord, do you wish to come into the house? Come in.'

Jesus stares at her as severe as a judge but does
not speak. But Judas does, supported by all the
others.

'Go back in, shameless woman! Do not desecrate
us with your breath, ravenous bitch.'

The woman blushes, bows her head and is about
to disappear abashed and scoffed at by urchins
and passers-by.

'Who is so pure as to say: "I have never desired the
apple offered by Eve?" ' Jesus asks,
severely. 'Show Me him and I will call him a holy
man. Nobody? Well, then, if not out of disgust, but
out of weakness, you feel unable to go near this
woman, you may withdraw. I will not force
weaklings into unequal struggles. Woman, I would
like to come in. This house belonged to a relative of
Mine and is dear to Me.'

'Come in, my Lord, if You do not loathe me.'

'Leave the door open, that the world may see and
may not tattle...'

Jesus enters, serious and solemn.

The woman, subdued, bows down before Him and
dares not move. But the quips of the people cut
her to the quick so she runs away to the end of the
garden, while Jesus goes as far as the foot of the
staircase. He looks in through the half open doors
but does not enter. Then He goes to the place
where the sepulchre once was, where there is now
a small pagan temple.

'The bones of the just, also when dry and
scattered, ooze a purifying balm and spread seed of
eternal life. Peace to the dead who lived doing good!
Peace to the pure who are sleeping in the Lord!
Peace to those who suffered, but knew no vice!
Peace to the real great ones of the world and of
Heaven! Peace! '

Walking along the protective hedge, the woman
has reached Jesus.

'My Lord! '
'Woman.'
'Your Name, my Lord.'
'Jesus. '
'I never heard it. I am Roman: a mime and dancer.
I am an expert only in lust. What is the meaning of
Your name? My name is Aglae and... and it means:
vice.'
'Mine means: Saviour.'
'How do You save? And whom?'
'Those who are anxious to be saved. I save by
teaching to be pure, to prefer sorrows to honours,
to desire good at all costs.' Jesus speaks without
bitterness, without even turning towards the
woman.
'I am lost...'
'I am the One seeking who is lost.'
'I am dead.'
'I am the One who gives Life.'
'I am filth and falsehood.'
'I am Purity and Truth.'
'You are also Bounty, You do not look at me. You
do not touch me, You do not tread on me. Have
mercy on me...'
'First, you must have mercy on yourself. On your
soul.'
'What is the soul?'
'It is what makes a god of man and not an animal.
Vice and sin kill it and once it is killed, man
becomes a repulsive animal.'
'Will it be possible for me to see You again?'
'Who looks for Me, finds Me.'
'Where do You live?'
'Where hearts need doctors and medicines to
become honest again.'
'In that case... I will not see You again... I live
where no doctor, medicine or honesty is wanted.'
'Nothing prevents you from coming to where I am.

My name will be shouted in the streets and will
reach you. Goodbye.'
'Goodbye, my Lord. Allow me to call You "Jesus".
Oh! Not out of familiarity!
... But that a little of salvation may come to me. I
am Aglae, remember me.'
'I will. Goodbye.'
The woman stays at the end of the garden whilst
Jesus comes out of it looking severe and a servant
closes the door. He looks at everybody, sees
perplexity in His disciples and hears jeers from the
Hebronites.
Walking straight along the road, Jesus knocks at
the synagogue and a resentful man looks out.
'The synagogue is forbidden, in this holy place, to
those who deal with prostitutes.
Go away.' says the man, not even giving Jesus time
to speak.
Without a reply, Jesus turns away and continues
walking along the road, followed by His disciples.

Outside Hebron, they begin to speak.
'You asked for trouble, Master ' says Judas. 'A
prostitute, of all people! '
'Judas, I solemnly tell you that she will surpass
you. And now, since you are reproaching Me, what
do you say of the Judaeans? In the most holy
places in Judaea we have been scoffed at and
driven away... That is the truth. The day will come
when Samaria and the Gentiles will worship the
true God, and the people of the Lord will be soiled
with blood and a crime... a crime in comparison
with which the sins of prostitutes who sell their
bodies and their souls, will be a very small thing. I
was not able to pray on the tomb of My cousins
and of the just Samuel. It does not matter. Rest,
holy bones, rejoice, souls, that dwelt in them. The
first resurrection is near. Then the day will come

when you will be shown to the angels as the souls of the servants of the Lord.'

Jesus At Kerioth. Death Of Old Saul.

Judas, Simon and John are with Jesus and they are walking through a valley between two mountain chains. They have left the shepherds behind, in the pastures of Hebron. The fields in this valley are not very large, but they are well cultivated with various cereals, mainly barley and rye and also some nice vineyards in the sunny parts. Higher up, there are lovely forests of Pine trees, fir trees and other trees typical of woody forests. A reasonably good road leads into a small village.

'This is the suburb of Kerioth. Please come to my country house. My mother is waiting for You there. We will go to Kerioth afterwards 'says Judas who is beside himself with excitement.

'As you wish, Judas, but we could have stopped even here to meet your mother. '

'Oh! No! It is only a farm house. My mother comes here at harvest time. But she lives in Kerioth. And do You not want my town people to see You? Do You not want to take Your light to them? '

'I certainly do, Judas. But you already are aware that I do not mind the humility of the place that gives Me hospitality. '

'But today You are my guest... and Judas knows how to be hospitable. '

They walk for a few more yards among houses spread about the country; men and women look out and children call, their curiosity awakened. Judas must have sent word to warn them.

'Here is my poor house. Forgive its poverty. '

But, the house is neither small nor squalid nor simply constructed. It consists of a large well-kept ground floor in the middle of a thick flowering orchard via a small clean private road leading from the main road to the house.

'May I go ahead of You, Master? '

'Yes, go. 'Judas goes.

'Master, Judas has done things in great style 'says Simon, 'I rather suspected he would. But now I am certain. Master, You keep saying, and quite rightly, spirit... But he... he does not see things that way. He will never understand You... or perhaps only very late 'he adds not to grieve Jesus. Jesus sighs and is silent.

Judas comes out with a woman of about fifty years old, rather tall, but not so tall as her son, who has her dark eyes and curly hair. But her eyes are kind and rather sad, whereas those of Judas are imperious and shrewd.

'I greet You, King of Israel 'she says prostrating herself in a real salutation of a subject. 'Allow Your servant to give You hospitality. '

'Peace to you, woman. And may God be with you and your creature. '

'Oh! yes! With my creature. 'She sighs.

'Stand up, mother. I have a Mother, too, and I cannot allow you to kiss My feet. I kiss you, woman, in My Mother's name. She is a sister of yours... in love and in the painful destiny of the mother of those who are marked. '

'What do You mean, Messiah? 'Asks Judas somewhat worried.

But Jesus does not reply. He is embracing the woman, whom He has kindly raised up from the ground and is now kissing her cheeks. And, holding her hand, He walks toward the house.

They go into a cool room, shaded by light striped curtains. Cold drinks and fresh fruit are already laid out. But first, Judas' mother calls a maidservant who brings in water and the landlady would like to take off Jesus' sandals and wash His dusty feet. But Jesus objects. 'No, mother. A mother is too holy a person, particularly when she is honest and good, as you are, to be allowed to take the attitude of a slave... '

The mother looks at Judas... an unusual look and then she goes away.

Jesus has refreshes Himself. When He is about to put on His sandals, the woman comes back with a new pair. 'Here, Messiah. I think I have done the right thing... as Judas wanted... He said to me: "A little longer than mine, but the same width."'

'But why, Judas? '

'Will You not let me offer You a gift? Are You not my King and my God? '

'Yes, Judas. But you must not give so much trouble to your mother. You know what I am like...
'

'I know. You are holy. But You must appear as a holy King. That is how one imposes oneself. – In the world, where nine tenths of the folk are foolish people, we must impose ourselves with our appearance. Trust me. '

Jesus has fastened the red leather open-work straps of the new sandals, which reach up to His ankles. They are much nicer than His plain sandals of a workman, and they resemble Judas' sandals, which are like shoes with open- work showing parts of his feet.

'Also the tunic, my King. I prepared it for Judas... But he makes a present of it to You. It's a linen one: cool and new. Allow a mother to put it on You... as if You were her son. '

Jesus looks at Judas once again... but does not speak. He unties the lace of His tunic, round His neck, and lets His wide tunic fall on to the floor and thus is left with only His short under-tunic. The woman puts on Him the lovely new garment. And then offers Him a richly embroidered braided belt with a hanging cord decorated with very thick tassels. Jesus must feel comfortable in the cool clean clothes, but He does not seem very happy. In the meantime the others have cleaned themselves.

'Come, Master. They come from my poor orchard. And this is honeyed water, prepared by my mother. Perhaps, Simon, you would prefer this white wine.

Have some. It is the wine of my vineyard. And what about you, John? Will you have the same as the Master? 'Judas is overjoyed as he pours the drinks into beautiful silver cups, thus showing his wealth.

His mother is not very talkative. She looks...
looks... at Judas, and even more at Jesus, and
when Jesus, before eating, offers her the nicest
fruit-yellow red in colour- and He says to her:

'First of all to mother, always ', her eyes well with
tears.

'Mother, is the rest ready? 'Asks Judas.

'Yes, son. I think I have done everything well. But I
was brought up here and I have always lived here
and I do not know... I do not know the habits of
kings. '

'Which habits, woman? Which kings? What have
You done, Judas? '

'Are You not the promised King of Israel? It is time
that the world should salute You as such, and that
must happen for the first time here, in my town, in
my house. I revere You as such. For my sake, and
for the respect due to Your names of Messiah,
Christ, King, which the Prophets gave You by
Yahweh's command, do not give me the lie. '

'Woman, friends, please. I must speak to Judas. I
have precise instructions to give him. '

The mother and the disciples withdraw.

'Judas: what have you done? Have you understood
so little of Me so far? Why lower Me to the extent of
making Me only a mighty man of the world, nay: a
man intriguing to become mighty? And do you not
understand that that is an offence, nay an obstacle
to My mission? Yes. Do not deny it. It is an

obstacle. Israel is subjected to Rome. You know what happened when they raised against Rome someone who seemed a mob-leader and aroused the suspicion of creating an insurrection. Only a few days ago you heard how pitiless they were against a Child because they were afraid He might be a king according to the world. And yet you!...

Oh! Judas! What do you expect from the sovereignty of the flesh? What do you expect? I gave you time to think and decide. I spoke to you very clearly from the very first time. I also sent you away because I knew... because I know, I read and see what is in you. Why do you want to follow Me, if you do not want to be as I want you? Go away, Judas. Do not harm yourself and do not harm Me... Go away. It is better for you. You are not a suitable worker for this task. It is by far too much above you. In you there is pride, there is greed and all its three branches, there is arrogance... even your mother must be afraid of you... you are inclined to falsehood... No, My follower must not be like that. Judas, I do not hate you, I do not curse you. I only say to you, and I am saying it with the grief of one who knows he cannot change the person he loves, I only say to you: go your way, make your way in the world, since that is what you want, but do not stay with Me.

My life!... My royal palace! How small and mean they are! Do you know where I will be a King? When I will be proclaimed King? When I will be raised up, upon an ill-famed piece of wood and My own blood will be My purple, and My crown will be a wreath of thorns and My insignia a mocking poster and the curses of all the people, of My people, will be the trumpets, the tambourines, the organs, the citherns saluting the proclamation of the King. And do you know by whose deed all this will happen? By the deed of one who did not understand Me. One who will have understood nothing. One, whose heart was a hollow piece of bronze, which pride, sensuality and avarice had filled with their humours, which will generate coils of snakes that will be used to chain Me and... and to curse him. The others are not so well aware of My destiny. Please do not tell them. Let us keep this to ourselves. In any case it is a reproach... and you will keep quiet to avoid saying: "I was reproached"... Is that clear, Judas? '

Judas has blushed so much, that he looks purple. He is standing before Jesus, mortified, his head lowered... He kneels down and he cries with his head on Jesus' knees: 'I love you, Master, Don't reject me. Yes, I am proud and foolish but don't send me away. No. Master. I will never do it again. You are right. It was thoughtless of me. But there is some love in my mistake. I wanted to honour You... and I wanted the others to honour You as well... because I love You. You said so three days ago: "When you make a mistake without malice, out of ignorance, it is not an error, but an imperfect judgement: like the error of children, and I am here to make adults of you." Here I am, here against Your knees... You said You would be a father to me... and I am here against Your knees as if they were my father's, and I ask You to forgive me, and to make an "adult" of me, a holy adult... Don't send me away, Jesus, Jesus, Jesus... Not everything is wicked in me. You know: I left everything for you and I have come. You are much more than the honours and victories I got serving other people. You are indeed the love of poor unhappy Judas who would like to give You nothing but joy, and is instead the cause of pain for You... '

69

'That is all right, Judas. I forgive you once again...
'Jesus looks tired... 'I forgive you, hoping... hoping
that in future you will understand Me. '

'Yes, Master. But, now, do not give me the lie,
otherwise I will be laughed at. Everybody in
Kerioth knows that I was coming with David's
Descendant, the King of Israel... and the town has
made preparations to welcome You... I thought I
was doing a good thing... showing You what one
must do to be respected and obeyed... and I also
wanted to show John and Simon, and through
them, all the others who love You but treat You as
their equal... Also my mother would be mocked at,
as the mother of a mad liar. For her sake, my
Lord... And I swear that I... '

'Do not swear to Me. Swear to yourself, if you can,
that You will not commit such a sin again. For the
sake of your mother and your fellow citizens I will
not shame you by going away without stopping
here. Stand up. '

'What will You tell the others? '

'The truth... '

'No, don't. '

'The truth: that I gave you instructions for today. It
is always possible to tell the truth in a charitable
way. Let us go. Call Your mother and the others. '

Jesus is rather severe. He smiles again only when
Judas comes back with his mother and the
disciples. The woman seems in great distress and

she gazes at Jesus but gains confidence when she sees His kind disposition.

'Shall we go to Kerioth? I have rested and I wish to thank you, mother, for all your kindness. May Heaven reward you and grant rest and peace to your late husband, for all your charity to Me. '

The woman tries to kiss His hand, but Jesus caresses her head and thus prevents her from doing so.

'The wagon is ready, Master. Come. '

Outside, in fact, an ox cart is just arriving. It is a comfortable cart, on which they have placed cushions as seats and a red tent as a cover.

'Get on, Master. '

'Your mother, first. '

The woman gets on and then Jesus and the others.

'Sit here, Master. ' (Judas no longer calls Him king).

Jesus sits in front, and Judas sits beside Him. The woman and the disciples are behind. The man driving the cart goads the oxen walking beside them.

It is a short journey; a little over four hundred meters. The first houses of Kerioth are now visible and it looks like a decent little town. A little boy who was watching on the sunny road immediately dashes away. When the cart reaches the first houses, the notables and the people welcome Him; the houses are decorated with draperies and branches. The people shout with joy and bow deeply. Jesus, from the height of His shaking throne, can but greet them and bless them.

The cart moves on and after crossing a square it turns into a street and stops before a house where the door is already wide open and two or three women are waiting at the door. They stop and get off. 'My house is Yours, Master. '

'Peace to it, Judas. Peace and holiness. '

They go in. Beyond the hall there is a large room, with low divans and inlaid furniture. The notables of the place and other people go in with Jesus. There is a lot of bowing and curiosity: a showy joyfulness. An impressive elderly man delivers a speech:

'It is a great honour for the land of Kerioth to receive You, my Lord. A great fortune! A happy day! It is a great fortune to have You and to see that a son of Kerioth is Your friend and assistant. May he be blessed because he met You before everyone else! And may You be blessed ten times ten because you have revealed Yourself: You are the one Who has been expected for generations and generations. Speak, my Lord and King. Our hearts are anxious to hear Your word, just as the land parched by a fiery summer awaits the first soft showers in September. '

'Thank you, whoever you are. Thank you. And thanks to these citizens whose hearts have honoured the Word of the Father, and the Father

Whose Word I am. Because You must understand that thanks and honour are due not to the Son of man, Who is speaking to you, but to the Most High Lord, for this time of peace during which He re-establishes the broken paternity with the sons of man. Let us praise the true Lord, the God of Abraham Who had mercy on and loved His people and granted them the promised Redeemer. Glory and praise not to Jesus, the servant of the Eternal Will, but to the loving Will. '

'Your words are the words of a holy man: I am the chief of the synagogue. To- day it is not a Sabbath. But come to my house, to explain the Law, since You are anointed with Wisdom, rather than with royal oil. '

'I will come. '

'Perhaps my Lord is tired... '

'No, Judas, I am never tired of speaking of God and I am never anxious to disappoint the hearts of men. '

'Come, then 'the synagogue chief insists. 'The whole of Kerioth is out there waiting for You. '

'Let us go. '

They go out. Jesus is between Judas and the arch synagogue, around them there are the notables and the crowds. Jesus passes through them blessing.

The synagogue is on the square. They go in. Jesus goes to the lectern. He begins to speak, bright in

His beautiful robes, His face inspired, His arms stretched out in His usual attitude.

'People of Kerioth, the Word of God is speaking to you. Listen. He Who is speaking to you is but the Word of God. His sovereignty comes from the Father and will return to the Father after Israel has been evangelized. May your hearts and minds be opened to the truth, so that you may be freed from errors and confusion.

Isaiah said: "For all the footgear of battle, every cloak rolled in blood, is burnt and consumed by fire. For there is a Child born to us, a Son given to us, and dominion is laid on His shoulders; and this is the name they give Him: Wonder-Counselor, Mighty-God, Eternal Father, Prince of Peace." That is My Name.

We leave to Caesar and the Tetrarchs their preys. I will commit a robbery. But not a robbery deserving to be punished by fire. On the contrary I will snatch from Satan's fire many of his preys and I will take them to the Kingdom of peace, of which I am the Prince, and to the future century: the eternal time of which I am the Father.

"God", says David, from whose stock I descend, as was prophesied by those who saw the future because of their holiness which was so pleasing to God, that He chose them as His messengers, "God elected one only... my son... but the work is great: this palace is not for man but for God." It is so. God, the King of kings, elected one person only: His Son, to build His house in the hearts of men. And He has already prepared the materials. Oh! How much gold of charity! And copper, silver, iron, rare wood and precious stones! They are all gathered in his Word Who makes use of them to build God's abode in you. But if man does not help the Lord, the Lord will build His dwelling place in vain. One must reply to gold with gold, to silver with silver, to copper with copper, to iron with iron.

That is, love is to be given for love, continence to serve Purity, perseverance to be loyal, strength to be steadfast. And one must carry stones today, wood tomorrow: a sacrifice today, a deed tomorrow and thus build. You must always build the Temple of God in your hearts.

The Master, the Messiah, the King of everlasting Israel and of God's eternal people, calls you. But He wants you to be pure for the work. Relinquish pride: praise is due to God. Relinquish human thoughts: the Kingdom belongs to God. Be humble and say with Me: "All things are Yours, Father. Everything that is good is Yours. Teach us how to know You and serve You in truth." Say: "Who am I?" And acknowledge that you will be something only when you become purified dwellings into which God may descend and rest.

You are all pilgrims and strangers in this world, learn how to gather together and proceed towards the promised Kingdom. The road: the commandments fulfilled not because of fear of a punishment, but out of love for You, holy Father. The Ark: a perfect heart in which the nourishing manna of wisdom is treasured and the branch of a pure will is certain to bloom. And come to the Light of the world, that your houses may be bright with light. I bring you the Light. Nothing else. I have no riches and I do not promise worldly honours. But I possess all the supernatural wealth of My Father and I promise the eternal honour of Heaven to those who will follow God with love and charity. Peace be with you. '

The people who have listened attentively, begin to murmur somewhat agitated. Jesus speaks to the head of the synagogue. Other people, perhaps the notables, join the group.

'Master, but are You not the King of Israel? We were told... '

'I am. '

'But You said... '

'That I neither possess nor promise worldly Wealth. I can speak but the truth. Yes, it is so. I know what you think. But the error is due to a misinterpretation and your great respect for the Most High. You were told: "The Messiah is coming" and you thought, like many in Israel, that Messiah and king were the same thing. Raise your minds higher up. Look at this beautiful summer sky. Do you think it ends there, where the air seems a sapphire vault? No, the most pure, the most azure spheres are beyond it, up as far as Paradise, which no one can imagine, where the Messiah will lead all the just who die in the Lord. The same difference exists between the Messiah's royalty, as understood by men, and His true Royalty: which is entirely divine. '

'But will we, poor men, be able to raise our minds so far up? '

'Yes, if you only want to. And if you want to, I will help you. '

'How shall we call You, if You are not a king? '

'Call Me Master, or Jesus, as you wish. I am a Master and I am Jesus, the Saviour. '

An old man says: ' Listen, my Lord. Some time ago, a long time ago, at the time of the edict, we heard here that the Saviour was born in Bethlehem... and I went there with other people... I saw a little Baby, exactly like all other new-born babies. But I adored Him with faith. Later I heard that there was a holy man, whose name is John. Which is the true Messiah? '

'The One you adored. The other is His Precursor: a great saint in the eyes of the Most High. But he is not the Messiah. '

'Was it You? '

'It was I. And what did you see around the new-born Child? '

'Poverty and cleanliness, honesty and purity... A kind grave carpenter, whose name was Joseph, a carpenter but of the House of David, a young mother, fair and kind, whose name was Mary, before whose grace the most beautiful roses of Engedi turns pale and the lilies of the royal flower beds seem misshapen, and a Child with large blue eyes and pale gold hair... I saw nothing else... And I can still hear the voice of the Mother say to me: "On behalf of My Creature I say to You: may the Lord be with you until the eternal meeting and

may His Grace come towards you on your way." I
am eighty-four years old... my way is near its end.
I was no longer expecting to meet the Grace of
God. Instead I have found You... and now I do not
wish to see any other light than Yours... Yes. I see
You as You are in this merciful attire, which is the
flesh You have taken. I see You! Listen to the voice
of a man who sees the Light of God while dying! '

The people press round the old inspired man, who
is in Jesus' group. No longer leaning on his
walking stick, he lifts his trembling arms and
raises his white head, which, with its by-parted
beard, seems the head of a patriarch or a prophet.

' I see Him: The Chosen, Supreme, Perfect One,
Who descended here out of love, I see Him rise
again to the right hand side of the Father and
become One with Him. But... Oh! He is not just a
Voice' or an incorporeal Essence, as Moses saw the
Most High, or as Genesis tells the First Parents
heard Him and spoke to Him in the evening breeze.
I see Him as real Flesh rising to the Eternal Father.
Blazing Flesh! Glorious Flesh! Oh! Pomp of Divine
Flesh! Oh! Beauty of the Man-God! He is the King!
Yes. The King. Not of Israel: of the world. All the
royalties of the earth bow to Him and all the
sceptres and crowns fade away in the splendour of
His sceptre and jewels. He has a crown on His
head and a sceptre in His hand. He wears a
rational on His chest: it is adorned with pearls and
rubies, the brightness of which was never seen
before. Flames issue from it as if it were a blazing
furnace. There are two rubies on His wrists and
buckles with rubies are on His holy feet. There is
so much light from the rubies! Admire, peoples,
the Eternal King! I see You! I see You! I am rising
with You... Ah!

Lord! Our Redeemer!... The light increases within my soul... The King is decorated with His own Blood! The crown is a wreath of bleeding thorns. The sceptre is a cross... Here is the Man! He is here! It is You!... Lord, for the sake of Your sacrifice have mercy on Your servant, Jesus, I commend my soul to Your mercy. ' The old man, who so far had stood up, rejuvenated by the fire of prophecy, suddenly collapses and would have fallen were Jesus not quick to hold him up against His chest.

'Saul. '

'Saul is dying! '

'Help! '

'Be quick. '

'Peace to the just man who is dying 'says Jesus, Who has slowly knelt down to support the old man, who has become heavier and heavier.

There is silence.

Then Jesus lays him down on the ground. And He stands up. 'Peace to his soul. He died seeing the Light. In his expectation which will be a short one, he will already see the face of God and will be happy. There is no death, that is parting from life, for those who died in the Lord. '

The people, after a little while, go away commenting. The elders, Jesus, His disciples and the archsynagogue remain.

'Did he prophesy, Lord. '

'His eyes saw the Truth. Let us go. 'They go out.

'Master, Saul died enraptured by the Spirit of God. We touched him, are we clean or unclean? '

'Unclean. '

'And what about You? '

'I am just like the others. I do not change the Law. The Law is law and an Israelite fulfils it. We are unclean. Within the third and the seventh day we shall get purified. Till then, we are unclean. Judas, I am not going back to your mother's. I do not want to take uncleanliness to her home. Send her word by someone who can go there. Peace to this town. Let us go. '

On His Way Back From Kerioth Jesus Stops With The Shepherds Near Hebron.

Jesus, with His disciples, is walking on a twisting road high up on the mountainside that plunges steeply down to a torrent on the valley floor. John is almost purple, laden like a porter, with a big heavy satchel, Judas is carrying Jesus' bag and his own and Simon has only his bag and the mantles. Jesus is now in his own clothes and sandals and the lack of creases on His tunic suggests that Judas' mother must have had it washed.

'How much fruit! How beautiful are those vineyards on those hills! 'Says John, who is always in good humour, notwithstanding the heat and the fatigue. 'Master, is this the river on the banks of which our fathers picked the miraculous grapes? '

'No, it is another one, farther south. But the whole region was blessed with rich fruit. '

'It is not so blessed now, although still beautiful. '

'Too many wars have devastated the country. Israel was made here... but it had to be fertilised by its own blood and by the blood of its enemies. '

'Where will we find the shepherds? '

'Five miles from Hebron, on the banks of the river you were enquiring about. '

'Beyond that hill, then. '

'Correct. '

'It's very warm. The summer... Where are we going after, Master? '

'To a place which is even warmer. But I ask you to come. We shall travel by night. The stars are so bright that there is no darkness. I want to show you a place... '

'A town? '

'No... A place... that will make you understand the Master... perhaps better than do His words. '

'We lost some days over that stupid incident. It spoiled everything... and my mother who had prepared so much, was disappointed. I cannot understand why You wanted to segregate Yourself with the purification... '

'Judas, why do you call stupid a fact that was a grace for a true believer? Would you not like such a death for yourself? He had waited all his life for the Messiah, and although an elderly man, he had gone along uncomfortable roads, to adore Him, when he was told: "He is here." He had kept My Mother's word for thirty years in his heart. He was enraptured by the fire of love and faith in the last hour granted to him by God. His heart burst out of joy and was burnt, like a pleasing holocaust, by the fire of God. Which destiny could be better? He spoiled the feast you had prepared? You can see in that the answer of God. The things of man are not to be mixed with the things of God... Your mother will have Me again. The old man would not have had Me again. The whole of Kerioth can come to Christ, the old man had no more strength to do so. I am happy that I held the old dying father against My heart and I commended his soul. With regard to the rest... Why give scandal lacking respect for the Law?

One must walk in front of the others if one wants to say: "Follow me." And to lead people on to a holy path, one must walk on the same path. How could I have said, or how could I say: "Be faithful", if I were faithless? '

'I think that error is the cause of our decay... 'Remarks Simon. '...The rabbis and Pharisees crush the people with their precepts and then... then they behave like the man who desecrated John's house, making it a place of sin. '

'He is one of Herod's... '

'Yes, Judas, but the same faults are to be found also in the classes which are said – by themselves of course – to be holy. What do you say about it, Master? 'Asks Simon.

'I say that only if there is a handful of true yeast and true incense in Israel, the bread will be made and the altar perfumed. '

'What do you mean? '

'I mean that if there is anyone coming to the Truth with a sincere heart, the Truth will spread like the yeast in the mass of flour and like incense all over Israel. '

'What did that woman say to You? 'Asks Judas. Jesus does not reply but, instead, addresses John: ' Your load is heavy and you are tired. Give it to Me. '

'No, Jesus, I am used to carrying weights and in any case... the thought of Isaac's joy makes it light. '

They go round the hillock. Elias' sheep are in the shade of the wood, on the other side. And the shepherds, sitting in the shade are watching them. When they see Jesus they start running.

'Peace to you. You are here? '

'We were worried about You... because of the delay... and we didn't know whether to come and meet You or obey... then we decided to come so far... and thus obey Your instructions and satisfy our love at the same time. You were to be here many days ago. '

'We had to stay... '

'Nothing... wrong? '

'No, My friends, nothing. A faithful believer died on My breast. Nothing else. '

'What do you think should have happened, shepherd? When things are well arranged...

Certainly one must know how to prepare them and prepare also hearts to receive them. My town paid every honour to Christ. Did they not, Master? '

'Yes, they did. Isaac, on our way back we called at Sarah's. Also the town of Juttah, without any preparation other than its simple goodness and the truth of Isaac's words, understood the essence of My doctrine and learned how to love with a holy practical unselfish love. She sent you some clothes and food, Isaac, and everybody wanted to add something to the alms you left on your bed, because you are now back in the world and you lack everything. Take this. I never take money. But I accepted this because it is purified by charity. '

'No, Master, You keep it. I... I am used to doing without it. '

'You will now have to go to the various villages, to which I will send you. And you will need it. A workman is entitled to his pay, also If he deals with souls... because there is still a body to be nourished, as if it were a donkey helping its master. It is not much. But you will manage. John has some clothes and sandals in that bag. Joachim took some of his own. They may be too big... but there is so much love in the gift! '

Isaac, who was still barefooted and wearing his strange gown made from a blanket, takes the bag and goes behind a bush to dress.

'Master 'says Elias. ' That woman... the woman who is in John's house... three days after You left and we were pasturing the sheep on the meadows of Hebron – they belong to everybody, the meadows, and they could not send us away – she sent her maid to us with this bag and told us that she wanted to speak to us... I don't know whether I did the right thing... but the first time I gave the bag back to her and said: "I do not want to listen to her"... Then she sent this message: "Come in Jesus' name" and I went. She waited until her... well, the man who keeps her, had gone... How many things she wanted to know. But I... didn't tell her very much. Out of prudence. She is a prostitute. I was afraid it might be a trap for You. She asked me who You are, where You live, what You do, if You are a gentleman... I said: "He is Jesus of Nazareth, He goes everywhere, because He is a Master, and He goes round Palestine teaching"; I said You are a poor man, a simple workman, made wise by Wisdom... Nothing else. '

'You did well 'says Jesus, whilst Judas, at the same moment, exclaims: 'You did the wrong thing! Why did you not say that He is the Messiah, the King of the world? The proud Roman woman should be crushed under the blow of God's splendour. '

'She would not have understood me... In any case how could I be sure that she was sincere? When you saw her, you said what she is. Was I to throw holy things, and everything that is Jesus is holy, into her mouth? Was I to endanger Jesus, giving too much information? Anyone may hurt Him, but I will not. '

'John, let us go and tell her who the Master is, and explain the holy truth to her.' Suggests Judas.

'Not me. Unless Jesus tells me. '

'Are you afraid? What can she do to you? Do you loathe her? The Master did not. '

'I am not afraid, neither do I loathe her. I feel sorry for her. But I think that if Jesus wanted, He could have stopped to teach her. He did not do it... it is not necessary for us to do it. '

'At the time there were no signs of a conversion... Now... Show me the bag, Elias. 'And Judas, who is sitting on the grass, empties the bag on his mantle. Rings, armlets, bracelets and a necklace roll out: yellow gold on the dark gold of Judas' mantle. 'They are jewels!... What can we do with them? '

'They can be sold 'says Simon.

'They are troublesome things 'says Judas but he admires them nonetheless.

'That's what I told her, when I took them; I also
said: "Your master will beat you." She replied:
"They do not belong to him. They are mine and I do
what I want with them. I know it is the gold of
sins... but it will become good if used for the poor
and the holy. That they may remember me" and
she was crying.'

'Go and see her, Master. 'Says Judas.

'No. '

'Send Simon. '

'No. '

'Well, I'll go. '

'No! 'Jesus' tone is sharp and peremptory.

'Was I wrong, Master, in speaking to her and taking that gold? 'Asks Elias, when he sees Jesus so serious.

'You did nothing wrong. But there is nothing more to be done. '

'But perhaps that woman wants to redeem herself and she needs to be taught...' Judas objects once again.

'There are already in her so many sparks capable of starting a fire which will burn her vices and purify her soul and repentance will render her innocent once again. A few minutes ago I spoke to you of the yeast which is mixed with the flour and turns it into holy bread. Listen now to a short parable.

That woman is the flour. A flour in which the Evil One has mixed his hellish powders. I am the yeast. That is, My word is the yeast. But if there is too much chaff in the flour, or if sand, or little stones or ashes are mixed in it, is it possible to make bread with it, even if the yeast is good? It is not possible. It is necessary to patiently remove the chaff, the ashes, stones and sand from the flour.

Then Mercy passes by and offers the first sieve... The first one: made with short basic truths, which may be understood by one entangled in the net of total ignorance, vice and paganism. If the soul accepts it, the first purification begins. The second takes place by means of the sieve of the soul itself, which compares its own being with the Being that revealed Itself. And the soul is horrified. And it starts its work by means of a more and more specific operation; after the stones, the sand and the ashes, it reaches the point of removing also that part of the flour consisting of grains too heavy and too coarse to make good bread. The soul is now ready. Mercy then passes by once again and penetrates into the flour now ready – that is a preparation too, Judas – and raises it and turns it into bread. But it is a long operation: an operation of the "will power" of the soul.

That woman already has in herself the minimum which was fair to give her and which may be used by her to accomplish her work. Let her do it, if she wishes to, but we must not disturb her. Everything upsets a soul which is working: curiosity, unadvised zeal, intolerance as well as excessive compassion. '

'We are not going to see her, then? '

'No. And that none of you may be tempted to, let us leave at once. There is shade in the wood. We will stop at the foot of the Terebinth Valley. And we will part there. Elias will go back to his pastures with Levi: Joseph will come with Me as far as the Jericho ford. Later... we will meet again. You, Isaac, continue what you did at Juttah, going from here, through Arimathaea and Lydda, to Doco. We will meet there. It is necessary to prepare Judaea, and you know how to do it. Exactly as you did at Juttah '.

'And what about us? '

'You? You will come, as I said, to see My preparation. Also I prepared for My mission. '

'Did You go to a rabbi's? '

'No. '

'Did You go to John? '

'I was only baptized by him. '

'Well, then? '

'Bethlehem spoke with its stones and its hearts. Also where I am taking you, Judas, the stones and a heart, Mine, will speak to you and give you the answer. '

Elias, who has brought some milk and brown bread, says: 'While waiting for You, I tried, and Isaac tried with me, to convince the people in Hebron... But they will not believe, they will not take an oath, they do not want anyone but John. He is their "holy man" and they do not want anyone else. '

'It is a sin quite common to many places and many present and future believers. They look at the workman, not at the master who sent the workman. They ask the workman questions and they do not even say to him: "Tell your master." They forget that there is a workman only because there is a master and that it is the master who instructs the workman and enables him to work. They forget that the workman can intercede, but only the master can concede. In this case God and His Word with Him. It does not matter. The Word is sorry but bears no grudge. Let us go. '

Jesus Returns To The Mountain Where He Fasted And To The Rock Of Temptation.

It is daybreak high up on a mountainside in the wilderness. A few stars are still visible and a very thin arc of a waning moon looks like a silver comma on the dark blue velvet of the sky. The mountain is completely isolated, that is, it is not linked to any other chain of mountains. The top of the mountain is much higher up, but even from the middle of its slope, which is well above ground level, one commands a very wide view of horizon. In the fresh morning air, as the faint white-greenish dawn light becomes clearer and clearer, profiles and details slowly emerge from the fog that precedes daybreak, a fog that is darker than night, because the light of the stars seems to diminish and fade away in the transition from night to day. The rocky barren face of the mountain emerges, split by gorges forming grottoes, caves and inlets. It is a real wilderness, with only a few green tufts of stiff thorny plants with few leaves and low hard bushes of wild desert grass with leaves like green stalks.

The plain below the mountain is even more barren; flat stony ground that becomes more arid as it stretches out towards a dark spot, much longer than it is wide, at least five times longer. In the dim morning light, it looks like a dense oasis that has sprung up in this bleakness from underground water but as the light becomes brighter, It reveals that it I nothing but stagnant, dark, dead water.

A lake of infinite sadness. In the still feeble light it conjures visions of a dead world and seems to be drawing to itself all the darkness of the sky and all the gloominess of the surrounding area, dissolving in its still waters the deep green of the thorny shrubs and stiff grass that for miles and miles around it and above it, are the only decoration on the face of the earth. And after filtering so much gloom it seems to spread it around once again. How different it is from the sunny, smiling lake of Gennesaret!

High above, looking at the clear blue sky, which now becomes clearer and clearer as the light progresses from the east in deeper and deeper brightness, one's soul rejoices. But looking at the huge, dead lake, gives one a stab in the heart. Not one bird flies over the water. Not one animal is on its shore. Nothing. Only desolation.

'Here we are at the place I wanted. ' says Jesus to John, Simon and Judas, who are near the rocky slope of the mountain, where the long erosion of waters, in the rainy months, has formed through the centuries, a very shallow channel, a drain for the water flowing from the mountain top and which is a path for wild goats rather than for men.

Jesus looks around and repeats: 'Yes, this is the place to which I wanted to bring you. Here Christ prepared for His mission. '

'But there is nothing here! '

'You are quite right, there is nothing. '

'With whom were You? '

'With My soul and with the Father. '

'Ah! You stayed only for a few hours! '

'No, Judas. Not a few hours. Many days... '

'But who served You? Where did You sleep? '

'My servants were the wild asses that came to sleep in their caves, where I, also, had taken shelter. My maidservants were the eagles that said to Me with their harsh cries: "It's daylight" and they flew away to attack their prey. My friends were the little hares that came up almost to My feet, gnawing at the wild herbs. My food and My drink were the same food and drink as of the wild flower: the night dew and the sunshine. Nothing else. '

'But why? '

'To prepare well, as you say, for My mission. Things that are well prepared for are successful. You said so yourself. And My thing was not a trifle, a useless thing that would glorify Me, the Servant of the Lord, but rather to make men understand what the Lord is, and by understanding, make Him loved in the spirit of truth. The servant that is concerned with his own triumph, and not with that of the Lord, is a miserable man! The servant who is anxious to make a profit, who dreams of sitting on a high throne built on the interests of God- celestial interests lowered down to the earth - is also a miserable servant. He is no longer a servant, except in outer appearance, but a merchant, a trafficker, a deceitful person, who deceives himself and men and would like to deceive also God... a wretched man who believes himself a prince whilst he is a slave. He belongs to the Evil One, his king of falsehood. Here, in this cave, Christ lived for many days, fasting and praying to get ready for His mission. And where would you have suggested I should have gone to prepare, Judas? '

Judas is puzzled and bewildered. Eventually he replies: 'I would not know... I was thinking... to a rabbi... or with the Essenes... I do not know. '

'And was it possible for Me to find a rabbi who would tell Me more than the power and wisdom of God were telling Me? And could I – I the Eternal Word of the Father, Who was present when the Father created man and am aware of the immortal soul by which he is animated and of the power of free capable judgement with which he was endowed by the Creator – would I have gone to derive science and skill from those who deny the immortality of souls, final resurrection and also the freedom of man to act? Who attribute virtues and vices, holy and wicked deeds to a destiny, which they say is fated and uncontrollable? Certainly not!

You have a destiny. In the mind of God Who creates you, there is a destiny for you. It is the wish of the Father. And it is a destiny of love, of peace, of glory: "the holiness of being His children." That is the destiny that was present in the divine mind when Adam was fashioned with dust and will be present until the creation of the last soul of man.

But the Father does not belittle you in your position of kings. If a king is a prisoner, he is no longer a king but an outcast. You are kings because you are free in your small individual kingdoms; your "ego". You can do what you like and how you like. Before you and on the boundaries of your small kingdom you have a friendly King and two enemy powers. The Friend shows you the rules that He gives to make His followers happy. He shows them and says: "Here they are. With them, your eternal victory is certain." He, The Wise and Holy One, shows them to you so that you may put them into practice, if you want to, and thus receive eternal glory.

The two enemy powers are Satan and the flesh. By flesh I mean your flesh and the world: they are the vain and ostentatious displays and enticements of the world; the riches, feasts, honours and powers which are obtained from the world and in the world, but are not always obtained honestly and are used even less honestly when eventually a man reaches them. Satan, the master of the flesh and of the world, speaks also on behalf of the world and of the flesh. He, too, has his rules... Oh! He certainly has! And as your "ego" is enveloped in the flesh, and the flesh is attracted by the flesh, as metal chips are attracted by a magnet, and the singing of the Seducer is sweeter than the moonlight warble of a nightingale in love among perfumed rose bushes, it is easier to follow those rules, and incline towards those powers and say to them: "I consider you my friends. Come in." Come in... Have you ever seen an ally who remains honest forever, without asking a hundredfold return for the help he has given? That is what those powers do. They go in... And they become the masters. Masters? No: galley sergeants.

They tie you, men, to the galley bench, they fasten you with chains, they do not allow you to raise your head from their yoke, and their lash leaves bleeding marks on your backs if you attempt to escape. You either must bear to be torn to pieces and become a heap of shattered flesh, so useless, as flesh, as to be rejected and kicked aside by their cruel feet, or you must die under their blows.

If you can bear that martyrdom, then Mercy will come, the Only One who can still have mercy on that revolting misery, which the world, one of the masters, now loathes and at which the other master, Satan, throws the arrows of his revenge. And Mercy, the Only One, passes by, bends down, picks it up, doctors it, cures it and says: "Come. Do not be afraid. Do not look at yourself. Your wounds are but scars, but they are so numerous that you would be horrified, as they disfigure you. But I do not look at them. I look at your good will. Because of your good will, you are marked. Therefore I say to you: I love you. Come with Me." And He takes it to His Country. You then understand that Mercy and the friendly King are the same person. You find the rules He had shown to you and you did not want to follow. Now you want them... and first you reach the peace of your conscience, then the peace of God. Tell Me, now. Was that destiny imposed by the Only One on everybody, or did each choose it for himself? '

'It was chosen by each person. '

'You are right, Simon. Was it possible for Me to go to those who deny the blessed resurrection and the gift of God, to be taught? I came here. I took My soul of the Son of man and I gave it its finishing touches and I thus finished the work of thirty years of humility and preparation in order to be perfect when starting My mission. Now I ask you to stay with Me for a few days in this cave. Our stay will be less depressing because we shall be four friends joining in our efforts against sadness, fears, temptation and the desires of the flesh. I was by Myself. It will be less painful, because it is now summer and up here, the mountain winds lessen the heat. I came here at the end of the Tebeth moon** and the wind blowing down from the snowy tops was harsh. It will be less trying because it will be shorter and also because we have the necessary food to satisfy our hunger and in the small leather flasks that I asked the shepherds to give you, there is enough water to last us for the days of our stay. I... I must snatch two souls from Satan. It can only be done by penance. I ask you to help Me. It will be a training for you. You will learn how to snatch victims from Mammon: not so much with words as with sacrifice... Words!... The satanic uproar prevents one from hearing them... Every soul which is a prey of the Enemy is enveloped in an eddy of infernal voices... Do you want to stay with Me? If you do not want to, you may go and we will meet at Tekoah, near the market. '

**The Tebeth moon is the tenth biblical lunar month equivalent to December/January

'No, Master, I will not leave You 'says John and Simon at the same time exclaims: 'You exalt us by wanting us to be with You in this redemption. '

Judas... does not appear to be terribly enthusiastic. But he puts on a good face and says: 'I will stay. '

'Well, take the flasks and the bags and put them inside, and before the sun gets hot, break some wood and gather it near the crevice. The nights are severe, even in summer, and not all the animals are gentle. Light a branch at once. Over there, a branch of that gummy acacia. It burns very well. We will search in the crevices and with the fire we will drive out asps and scorpions. Go. '...

... It is night time on the mountainside beneath a starry sky so clear and bright, it looks tropical; the stars are wonderfully large and bright. The bigger constellations seem clusters of diamond chips, of clear topazes, of pale sapphires, of mild opals and soft rubies that tremble, light up and twinkle like glances hidden for an instant by eyelashes, and then light up again more beautiful than before. Now and again a star swoops across the sky in a streak of light like a jubilant cry of a star flying over wide landscapes and disappears in the horizon.

Jesus is sitting at the entrance of the cave and talking to the three disciples who are sat in a circle round Him. In their midst, bright embers from a dying fire cast their ruddy glow on the four faces.

'Yes. Our stay is over. My last stay here lasted forty days... And I would repeat that it was still winter up here... and I had no food. A little more difficult than this time, was it not? I know that you have suffered even now. The little food I gave you was nothing, particularly for hungry young people. It was barely sufficient to prevent you from collapsing. And the water even less so. The heat is intense during the day. And you will say that it was not so in winter. But then there was a dry wind blowing from that mountain top and it parched My lungs. It rose from the plain loaded with desert dust and it dried more than this summer heat which can be relieved by sucking the juice of those sour fruits that are almost ripe. The mountain in winter gave only wind and frost-bitten herbs near bare acacias. I did not give you everything because I kept the last bread and cheese and the last flask of water for our way back... I know what My return journey was like, exhausted as I was in the desert solitude... Let us pick up our things and go. Tonight is even clearer than the night we came here; there is no moon but light is pouring from the sky. Let us go. Remember this place. Remember how Christ prepared and how the apostles prepare. Let the apostles prepare as I teach them. '

They get up. Simon stirs the embers with a stick, throws some dry herbs on them to rekindle the fire from which he then lights a branch of acacia and holds it up at the entrance of the cave whilst Judas and John pick up mantles, bags and small leather flasks of which only one is still full. Then he rubs the branch against the rock to put out the flame, scatters the remaining embers with his foot, takes his satchel, puts on his mantle like the rest of them and ties it at the waist so that it would not hinder him in walking.

Without speaking, one behind the other, they go down a very steep path, sending small animals grazing on the scanty grass scurrying beneath the sparse sun scorched bushes. It is a long and uncomfortable descent but at last they reach the plain. Even here, stone and stone splinters concealed beneath the thick layer of dust undermine the feet, causing them to slide suddenly, sometime hurting themselves as unseen, the splinter and stones are impossible to avoid. Progress is slow. Further along, naked thorny bushes scratch and catch the lower part of their garments but here at least they can walk faster. High above, the stars grow lovelier and lovelier.

They walk for hours, the plain becoming more and more barren and depressing. Little scales like dirty scales of diamond chips sparkle in small crevices and holes in the ground and John bends down to look at them.

'It is the salt of the subsoil which is saturated with them. It seeps to the surface with the spring waters and then dries up. That is why life is impossible here. The Eastern Sea spreads its death for many miles around, through deep veins in the ground. Only where fresh spring waters counteract its effects, is it possible to find plants and ease 'explains Jesus.

They go on walking. Jesus stops at the hollow rock where He was tempted by Satan. 'Let us stop here. Sit down. It will soon be daybreak. We have walked for six hours and you must be hungry, thirsty and tired. Take this. Eat and drink, sitting here, near Me, while I tell you something that you will repeat to your friends and to the world. '

Jesus opens His satchel and pulls out bread and cheese, which He cuts and hands out. From His flask He pours out some water into a small jug and He hands it round, too.

'Are You not eating, Master? '

'No, I will speak to you. Listen. Once a man asked Me whether I had ever been tempted. He asked Me whether I had ever committed a sin, and whether, when tempted, I had ever given in. And he was surprised because, in order to resist temptation, I, the Messiah, had asked the Father for help, saying: "Father, lead Me not into temptation."...'

Jesus speaks slowly, calmly as One relating an event with which none of them were acquainted... Judas bows his head as one embarrassed but the others are so intent on looking at Jesus, that they do not notice him.

'... Now, My friends, you will learn something about which that man had only a faint idea. After My Baptism I came here: I was clean, but one is never clean enough with regard to God, and the humility in saying: "I am a man and a sinner" is already a baptism that makes the heart clean. I had been called "the Lamb of God" by the holy prophet who saw the Truth and saw the Spirit descend upon the Word and anoint Him with its chrism of love, whilst the voice of the Father filled the Heavens saying: "This is My beloved Son in Whom I am well pleased." You, John, were present when the Baptist repeated those words... After being baptized, although I was clean both by My nature and by appearance, I wanted to "prepare". Yes, Judas. Look at Me. May My eyes tell you what My mouth does not yet speak. Look at Me, Judas. Look at your Master, Who although was the Messiah, did not consider Himself superior to man. On the contrary, knowing He was the Man, He wanted to be so in everything, except in yielding to evil. Exactly so. '

Judas, now with head raised, looks at Jesus in front of him. The light of the stars causes Jesus' eyes to sparkle like two stars fixed in a pale face.

'If one wants to prepare to be a teacher, one must have been a pupil. I, as God, knew everything. My intelligence enabled Me to understand also the struggles of man, both by intellectual power and in an intellectual way, that is without any practical experience. But then some poor friend of Mine, some poor son of Mine, could have said to Me: "You do not know what it is to be a man and have senses and passions." And it would have been a fair reproach. I came here, or rather on that mountain, to prepare... not only for My mission... but also for temptation. See? I was tempted where you now sit. By whom? By a mortal being? No. His power would have been too limited. I was tempted by Satan himself.

I was exhausted; I had not eaten for forty days... But while I was engrossed in prayer, everything had been forgotten in the joy of speaking to God-or rather not forgotten but made endurable. I felt it as a discomfort of a material nature, confined to matter only... then I came back to the world... I was back in the ways of the world... And I felt the needs of those who are in the world: hunger, thirst and the biting cold of the desert night. My body was worn out with lack of rest, want of a bed and from a long journey made in such a state of weariness that I could go no farther...

Because I am made of flesh too, My dear friends-
real flesh-My flesh is subject to the weakness
common to all the flesh. And, with My flesh, I have
a heart. Yes, I took the first and second of the
three parts that form man. I took the physical part
with all its needs and the morals with their
passions. And whilst, with My will, I subdued all
the bad passions at birth, I let the holy passions
grow like mighty age-old cedars, that is filial love,
love for the fatherland, friendship, work, everything
that is best and holy. And here I felt nostalgia for
My far away Mother, here I felt the need of Her care
for My human frailty, here I felt once again the
pain of parting from the Only One Who loved Me
with perfect love, here I realized what sorrow is laid
aside for Me and I was grieved at Her sorrows, poor
Mother, Who will have to shed so many tears for
Her Son and because of the wickedness of men,
that She will be left tearless. And here I
experienced the weariness of the hero and of the
hermit who in an hour of forewarning realize the
uselessness of their efforts... I cried... Sadness... a
lure for Satan. It is not a sin to be sad in painful
circumstances. It is a sin to go beyond sadness
and fall into **slothfulness** and despair.

But Satan comes at once when he sees anyone in
spiritual languor.

He came. Dressed as a kind traveller. He always
takes a kind appearance... I was hungry... and
thirty years old. He offered to help Me. First he
said to Me: "Tell these stones to become bread."
But before... yes... even before, he spoke to Me
about woman. Oh! He knows how to speak of her.
He knows her very well. He corrupted her first, to
make her his ally in corruption. I am not only the
Son of God. I am Jesus, the workman of Nazareth.

I said to that man, who was speaking to Me then, the one who asked Me whether I had experienced temptations and almost accused Me for being unjustly blessed, because I had not sinned: "The act subsides when satisfied. A rejected temptation does not fade away, but becomes stronger also because Satan instigates it." I resisted the temptation both of **lust** of woman and hunger for bread. And you must know that Satan proposed woman to Me as the best ally to succeed in the world, and he was quite right, from a human point of view.

Temptation did not give up because of My remark: "Man does not live on his senses only" and he spoke to Me of My mission. He wanted to seduce the Messiah after failing with the young Man. And he incited Me to crush the unworthy ministers of the Temple with a miracle... A miracle, the fire of Heaven, is not to be bent to form a wicker wreath to crown ourselves... And we must not put God to the test, asking for miracles for human purposes. That is what Satan wanted. The reason mentioned by him was an excuse; the truth was: "Boast of being the Messiah", as he wanted to lead Me to another lust: the lust for **pride**. He was not daunted by My reply: "You must not put the Lord your God to the test" and he circumvented Me with the third power of his nature: gold. Oh! gold. Bread is a great thing, and woman an even greater one for those longing for food or pleasure. To be acclaimed by the crowds is a very great thing for man. How many crimes are committed for these three things! But gold... gold! It is a key that opens, a circle that joins, it is the beginning and end of ninety-nine of human actions. For bread and a woman man becomes a thief. For power he becomes also a murderer. But for gold he becomes an **idolator.**

The king of gold, Satan, offered Me his gold if I adored him. I pierced him with the eternal words: "You shall worship the Lord your God, and serve Him only." It happened here. '

Jesus is now standing and seems taller than usual in the flat nature that surrounds Him, in the slightly phosphorescent light of the stars. Also the disciples get up. Jesus goes on speaking, staring intently at Judas.

'Then the angels of the Lord came... The Man had won the treble battle. The Man knew what it meant to be a man and had won. He was exhausted. The struggle had been more exhausting than the long fast... But the spirit was triumphant... I think that Heaven was startled at My becoming a perfect creature endowed with knowledge. I think that from that moment I got the power of working miracles. I was God. I had become the Man. Now, by defeating the animal nature connected with man's nature, I was the Man-God. And I am. And as God I am omnipotent. And as Man I am omniscient. Do as I did, if you want to do what I do. And do it in memory of Me.

That man was amazed at My asking the Father's help, and at My praying not to be led into temptation. That is, not to be left at the mercy of temptation beyond My strength. I think that that man will no longer be amazed, now that he knows. I ask you to do the same in My memory and to win as I did. And never doubt My nature of true Man and true God, seeing how strong I was in all the temptations of life, and how I won the battles of the five senses, of sensuality and of sentiments. Remember all that. I promised to take you where it would be possible for you to know the Master... from the dawn of His day, a dawn which is as pure as the one which is now rising, to the noontide of His life. The noon which I left to go and meet My human evening... I said to one of you: "I also prepared"; you now see it is true. I thank you for your company in the return to the place of My birth and the place of My penance. My first contacts with the world had sickened and depressed Me. It is too ugly. My soul has now been nourished with the lion's marrow: the union with the Father in prayer and solitude. And I can go back to the world and take My cross upon Me once again, the first cross of the Redeemer: the cross of the contact with the world. With the world, in which there are too few souls called Mary, called John... Now listen, and you in particular, John. We are going back towards My Mother and our friends. I beg you not to mention to My Mother the harshness which has been opposed to the love of Her Son. She would suffer too much. She will suffer so much because of man's cruelty... but do not let us give Her the chalice now. It will be so bitter when it is given to Her! So bitter that it will creep like poison into Her holy viscera and veins and will gnash them and freeze Her heart. Oh!

Do not tell My Mother that Bethlehem and Hebron rejected Me like a dog! Have mercy on Her! You, Simon, are old and good, and thoughtful as you are, you will not speak, I know. You, Judas, are a Judaean, and will not speak out of patriotic pride. But you, John, are a Galilean, and young, do not commit a sin of pride, criticism and cruelty. Be silent. Later... later you will tell the rest what I now ask you to be silent about. There is already so much to be said about Christ. Why add to it what is Satan's work against Christ? My dear friends, do you promise Me that? '

'Oh! Master! We do promise. Be certain of it. '

'Thank you. Let us go to that small oasis. There is a spring, a well full of cold water and there is shade and greenery. The road towards the river passes near it. We will find food and refreshment till evening. By starlight, we will reach the river, the ford. And we will wait for Joseph or join him if he is already back. Let us go. '

They set out as the first pinkish hue in the eastern sky announces the rising of a new day.

At The Jordan Ford. Meeting With The Shepherds John, Matthias And Simeon.

There are lines of little donkeys and people coming and going along the beaten road that runs along the green banks of the Jordan. Also on the river bank, are three men guarding a few sheep in the pasture.
Joseph is waiting on the road, looking up and down. In the distance, at the junction of the river path with the main road, Jesus appears with His three disciples. Josephs calls out to the shepherds who driving the sheep along the grassy bank, walk fast towards Jesus.

'I haven't got the courage... What shall I say to greet Him? '
'Oh! He is so good! Say: "Peace be with You." He always says that. '
'Yes, He... but we... '
'And what about me? I am not even one of His first worshippers and He is so fond of me... oh! so fond!
'
'Which one is it? '
'The tallest One, with fair hair.'
'Matthias, will we tell Him of the Baptist?'
'Of course we will! '
'Will He not think that we preferred the Baptist to

Him? '
'No, Simeon. If He is the Messiah, He can see into
the hearts of men and in ours He will see that in
the Baptist we were still looking for Him.'
'Yes, you are right.'

With the two groups now only a few yards apart,
the shepherds can see Jesus smiling at them with
His indescribable smile and Joseph hastens his
step. The sheep, urged by the herdsmen, also
begin to run.

'Peace be with you ' says Jesus raising His arms in
a wide embrace. 'Peace to you, Simeon, John and
Matthias, faithful to Me, and faithful to John the
Prophet!...' He adds specifically to each of the
shepherds who are now down on their
knees. '...Peace to you, Joseph ' and He kisses him
on his cheeks. 'Come, My friends. Under these
trees on the exposed river-bed and let us talk. '

They go down to the exposed riverbed where Jesus
sits on a large protruding root and the others on
the ground. Jesus smiles and looks at them
intently, one by one: 'Let Me become familiar with
your faces. Your souls are already known to Me,
souls that seek and love what is good contrary to
all worldly yearnings. Isaac, Elias and Levi send
you their regards and there are other greetings
from My Mother. Have You any news of the
Baptist? '

The men, so far gagged by embarrassment, take
heart and find words at last: 'He is still in jail. Our
hearts tremble for him because he is in the hands
of a cruel man who is dominated by an infernal
creature and is surrounded by a corrupt court. We
love him... You know that we love him and that he

deserves our love. After you left Bethlehem, we were persecuted by men... but we were distressed and disheartened because we had lost You, rather than by their hatred, and we were like trees uprooted by the wind. Then, after years of suffering, like a man whose eyelashes have been stitched struggles to see the sun, but cannot, also because he is closed in a prison but feels the warmth of the sun on his body, we felt that the Baptist was the man of God foreseen by the Prophets to prepare the way to His Christ and we went to him. We said: "If the Baptist precedes Him, if we go to the Baptist, we will find Him." Because, my Lord, it was You we were looking for. '

'I know. And you found Me. And now I am with you. '
'Joseph told us that You came to the Baptist. But we were not there that day. Perhaps he had sent us somewhere. We serve him in spiritual matters, when he asked us, with so much love. And we listened to him with love, although he was so severe, because he was not You – the Word – but he always spoke words of God.'

'I know. And do you know this man? ' Jesus asks, pointing to John.
'We saw him with the other Galileans in the crowds which were most faithful to the Baptist. And, if we are not mistaken, you are the one whose name is John, and of whom he used to say to us, his closest disciples: "Here: I am the first, he is the last. And then: he will be the first and I the last." But we never understood what he meant.'

Jesus turns to John on His left and He draws him against His heart and with a most kind smile He explains: 'He meant that he was the first to say:

113

"Here is the Lamb" and that John here will be the last of the friends of the Son of man to speak of the Lamb to the crowds; but that in the heart of the Lamb, John is the first, because he is dearer than any other man to the Lamb. That is what he meant. But when you see the Baptist – You will see him again, and you will serve him again until the predetermined hour – tell him that he is not the last in Christ's heart. Not so much because of the blood, as on account of his holiness, he is loved as much as John. And remember that. If the saint in his humility proclaims himself "last", the Word of God proclaims him equal to the disciple who is dear to Me.. Tell him that I love this disciple because he has the same name and because I find in him the signs of the Baptist, who prepares the souls for Christ.'

'We will tell him... But will we see him again? '
'Yes, you will. '
'Yes, Herod dare not kill him for fear of the people and at his court, which is full of greed and corruption, it would be easy to free him if we had a lot of money. But, although there is quite a lot – because friends have given a lot – there is still a lot missing. And we are afraid we will not be in time... and he may be killed. '
'How much do you think you need for the ransom? '

'Not for his ransom, Lord. Herodias hates him too much and she has too much control of Herod to allow the possibility of a ransom. But I think that all the greedy people of the kingdom have gathered at Machaerus. Everybody is anxious to have a good time and stand out; from the ministers down to the servants. And to do that, they need money... We have also found who would let the Baptist out for a large sum of money. Perhaps also Herod would prefer that... because he is afraid. Not for any other reason. He is afraid of the people and afraid of his wife. In that way, he could please the people and his wife could not accuse him of disappointing her.'

'And how much does that person want? '

'Twenty silver talents. But we have only twelve and a half.'

'Judas, you said that those jewels are beautiful. '

'Yes, beautiful and valuable.'

'How much will they be worth? I think you are an expert.'

'Yes, I am a good judge. Why do You want to know how much they are worth, Master? Do You want to sell them? Why? '

'Perhaps... Tell Me: how much will they be worth? '

'At least six talents, if they are sold well. '

'Are you sure? '

'Yes, Master. The necklace by itself, so big and
heavy, of the purest gold, is worth at least three
talents. I have examined it carefully. And also the
bracelets... I don't know how Aglae's thin wrists
could hold them. '
'They were her shackles, Judas.'
'That's true, Master... But so many would like to
have such beautiful shackles!'
'Do you think so? Who? '
'Well... many people! '
'Yes, many who are human beings only by name...
And do you know a possible buyer? '
'So, do You want to sell them? And is it for the
Baptist? But look, it's cursed gold! '
'Oh! Human inconsistency! You have just said with
evident desire, that many people would love to

have that gold, and then you say it is cursed?!
Judas, Judas!... It is cursed, indeed. But she said:
"It will be sanctified if it is used for poor and holy
people" and that is why she gave it, that who
benefits by it, may pray for her poor soul that like
the embryo of a future butterfly swells in the seed
of her heart. Who is holier and poorer than the
Baptist? He is equal to Elijah in his mission but
greater than Elijah in holiness. He is poorer than I
am. I have a Mother and a home... And when one
has such things, and pure and holy as I have, one
is never forlorn. He no longer has a home, and he
has not got even the tomb of his mother.
Everything has been violated and desecrated by
human iniquity. So who is the buyer? '
'There is one in Jericho and there are many in
Jerusalem. But the one in Jericho!!! He is a shrewd
Levantine gold-beater, a loan shark, a middleman,
a pander, he is certainly a thief. Probably a killer.
He is definitely persecuted by Rome. He has
changed his name to Isaac, to pass for a Hebrew...
But his real name is Diomedes. I know him very
well... '
'Yes, we see that!... 'intervenes Simon Zealot, who
speaks little, but notices everything.'...How come
you know him so well? '
'Well... you know... In order to please certain
mighty friends. I went to see him... and did some
business... You know... we of the Temple... '
'I know... you do all sorts of jobs ' concludes Simon
with cold irony. Judas flares up, but keeps silent.
'Will he buy? ' asks Jesus.
'I think so. He has plenty money. Of course, one
must be skilful in selling because the Greek is
shrewd and if he realizes he is dealing with an
honest person, with a nestling dove, he plucks him
mercilessly. But if he has to deal with a vulture
like himself...'

'You ought to go, Judas. You are the right man.
You are as sly as a fox and as predatory as a
vulture. Oh! Forgive me, Master. I spoke before
You! ' says Simon Zealot again.
'I am of the same opinion, and I will therefore tell
Judas to go. John, you will go with him. We will
meet again at sunset and the meeting place will be
the market square. Go. And do your best.'
Judas gets up at once and John turns his
imploring chastened puppy's eyes on Jesus, who,
speaking to the shepherds, does not notice so John
sets out behind Judas.

'I would like to see you happy ' says Jesus.
'You will always make us happy, Master. May God
bless You for it. Is that man a friend of Yours? '
'Yes, he is. Do you think he should not be? '
The shepherd John lowers his head, and keeps
silent but Simon speaks: 'Only who is good, can
see. I am not good, and therefore I do not see what
Bounty sees. I see the exterior. Who is good
penetrates also into the interior. You, John, see as
I do. But the Master is good... and sees... '
'What do you see in Judas, Simon? I want you to
tell Me.'
'Well, when I look at him, I think of certain
mysterious places that look like dens of wild beasts
and malaria infested ponds. One can only see a
huge tangle and, frightened, one keeps clear...
Instead... behind it there are turtle-doves and
nightingales and the soil is rich in healthy waters
and good herbs. I want to believe that Judas is like
that... I think he must be, because You chose him.
And You know... '
'Yes, I know... There are many flaws in the heart of
that man... But he has some good points. You saw
that yourself in Bethlehem and in Kerioth. And his

good points which are humanly good are to be raised to a spiritual goodness. Judas will then be as you would like him to be. He is young... '

'Also John is young... '

'And in your heart, you conclude that he is better. But John is John! Love poor Judas, Simon, I beg you.. If you love him... he will appear to be better. '

'I try to love him for Your sake. But he breaks all my efforts as though they were water canes... But, Master, there is only one law for me: to do what You want. I will, therefore, love Judas although something within me shouts out to me against him'

'What, Simon? '

'I do not know exactly what it is: something that resembles the cry of the night watchman... and says to me: "Do not sleep! Watch!" I do not know. That something has no name. But it is here... in me, against him. '

'Forget about it, Simon. Do not trouble to give it a definition. It is better not to know certain truths... and you might be mistaken. Leave it to your Master. Give Me your love and you can be sure that it makes Me happy... '

Judas Iscariot Tells Of How He Sold Aglae's Jewels To Diomedes.

It is sunset on a very warm summer day at the market place in Jericho. But for a few passers-by, some women going to the fountain and some quarrelsome children dressed in rags and throwing stones at the birds perched in the trees, the marketplace is empty. Remains of vegetables, heaps of excrement, straw fallen from donkeys' baskets and rags, all fermenting in the heat of the sun and covered with flies- are all that is left of the morning's market.

Arriving onto the square via a side street, Jesus looks around and seeing no one, waits patiently, leaning against a tree trunk. Whilst He waits, he speaks to the boys about charity that begins with God and from Him, the Creator, descends to all creatures.

'Do not be cruel. Why do you want to annoy the birds of the air? They have their nests up there, and their little ones. They harm no one. They give us their chirping and cleanliness, because they eat the rubbish left by men and the insects that are harmful to crops and fruit. Why wound them, or kill them, depriving the little ones of their fathers and mothers, or the parents of their little ones? Would you be glad if a wicked man came to your house and destroyed it, or killed your parents, or took you away from them? No, you would not be happy. Well, then, why do to these innocent creatures what you would not like done to yourselves? How will you, refrain one day from doing harm to men if, children as you are now, you harden your hearts, and hurt defenceless, kind little creatures such as these birds? Do you not know that the Law says: "Love your neighbour as yourself"? Who does not love his neighbour does not love God. And who does not love God, how can he go to His House and pray to Him? God might say to him, and he does say it in Heaven: "Go away. I do not know you.

You, My son? No, you are not. You do not love your brothers, you do not respect in them the Father Who created them, so you are not a brother and a son, but an illegitimate child: a stepson to God, a stepbrother to your brothers." See how the Eternal Lord loves? In the cold months, He makes His little birds find the barns full of hay, so that they may nest there. In the hot months, He protects them from the sun with the foliage of trees. In winter the corn in the fields is just covered with earth and it is easy for them to find the seed and nourish themselves. In summer they quench their thirst with the juice of fruits, and they build solid, warm nests with hay and the wool left on brambles by sheep. And He is the Lord. You, little men, created by Him like the little birds, and therefore their brothers in creation, why do you want to differ from Him and think that you can be cruel to these little animals? Be merciful with everybody, not depriving anyone of what is due to one: both amongst men and animals, your servants, your friends and God... '

'Master? ' calls Simon ' Judas is coming. '

'... and God will be merciful with you, and will give you everything you need, as He does with these innocent creatures. Go and take the peace of God with you.'

Jesus makes His way through the boys and some of the adults who had joined them, and goes towards Judas and John, who are coming from another street. Judas is jubilant. John smiles at Jesus... but does not seem very happy.

'Come, come, Master. I think I have done well. But come with me. It is not possible to speak here in the street.'

'Where, Judas? '

'To the hotel. I have already booked four rooms... oh! nothing special, don't worry. Only to rest in a bed after so much discomfort in all this heat, and to have a meal like men and not like birds perched on branches, and also to talk in peace. I sold the jewels very well, didn't I, John? '

John nods in assent but not very enthusiastically. But Judas is too pleased with his work to notice that Jesus is not very happy at the prospect of comfortable lodgings or that John is less than enthusiastic about his transactions.

'As I had sold at a higher price than I had estimated, I said: "It is fair that I should take a small amount, one hundred coins, for our beds and meals. If we are exhausted, although we always had something to eat, Jesus must be completely worn out." I am obliged to ensure that my Master is not taken ill! An obligation of love, because You love me, and I love You... There is room also for you and the sheep 'he says to the shepherds. 'I have seen to everything. '

Jesus does not say one word, but follows Judas, as do the others.

They arrive in a smaller square.

'See that house without any windows opening on the street and with the narrow little door that looks like a fissure?...' directs Judas '... It's Diomedes, the goldbeater's house. It looks like a poor house, doesn't it? But there is enough gold in there to buy the whole of Jericho and... Ah! Ah!...' Judas laughs maliciously '... amongst all that gold, there are many jewels and plates, as well as other things, belonging to the most influential people in Israel. Diomedes... oh! They all pretend they do not know him but they all do: from the Herodians down to... to everybody. On that plain, smooth wall, one could write: "Mystery and Secret". If those walls could speak!...'

'.... Then you would not be scandalized at the way I
negotiated this business, John! You... you would
die, choked with amazement and scruples. By the
way, listen, Master. Never send me again with
John on certain business. He almost ruined
everything. He cannot take a hint, he cannot deny
things, whereas with shrewd men like Diomedes
one must be quick and outspoken. '

John grumbles: 'You were saying certain things. So
unexpected and so... so... Yes, Master. Do not send
me again. I am only good at being kind and
loving... I... '

'It is most unlikely that we shall ever need such transactions again.' Replies Jesus, very seriously.

'That is the hotel over there. Come, Master. I will do the talking, because I arranged everything. '

They go in, and Judas speaks to the landlord, who has the sheep taken to a stable whilst he takes the guests into a little room with two mat-beds, some chairs and a table already laid out. Then he withdraws.

'I will tell you what happened at once, Master, while the shepherds are settling the sheep.'

'I am listening.'

'John can say whether I am telling the truth.'

'I do not doubt it. No oath or witness is required among honest men. Tell Me.'

'We arrived in Jericho at midday, wet with perspiration, like pack- animals. I did not want to give Diomedes the impression that I was in urgent need. So first of all, I came here, refreshed myself, put on clean clothes, and got John to do the same. Oh! He would not hear of having his hair sorted and perfumed. But I had made out my plans on my way here!... When it was almost evening, I said: "Let's go." By then, we were well rested and fresh like two wealthy people on a pleasure trip. When we were about to arrive at Diomedes' house, I said to John: "Always agree to what I say. Do not contradict me, and be quick to take a hint." But I should have left him outside! He did not help at all.

Quite the contrary... Fortunately, I am as quick as two people, and I managed.

The excise man was coming out of his house. "Very well!" I said. "If he is coming out, we will find the money and what I need to make a comparison." Because the excise man, being a loan shark and a thief like all his kind, always has necklaces seized with threats and extortion from the poor people whom he taxes more than is fair, in order to have plenty to spend in feasting and women. And he is very friendly with Diomedes, who buys and sells gold and flesh... We went in after I had made myself known. I said: we went in. Because there is a difference between going into the entrance hall, where he pretends to be doing an honest job, and going down into the basement, where he does his real business. One must be well known to him to be introduced there. As soon as he saw me, he said: "Do you want to sell more gold? We are going through hard times, and I have little money." His usual old story. I replied: "I have not come to sell, but to buy. Have you any jewels for a lady? But they must be beautiful, valuable, heavy, in pure gold!" Diomedes was amazed. And he asked me: "Do you want a woman?" "Never mind that" I replied to him. "They are not for me. They are for this friend of mine who is getting married and wishes to buy the jewels for his beloved bride."

At this point, John began to behave like a child. Diomedes, who was looking at him, saw him turn purple, and being a filthy old man, he said: "Ah! The boy has only heard his bride mentioned and he is in heat. Is your woman very beautiful?" he asked. I kicked John to rouse him, and to make him understand not to behave foolishly. But he replied "Yes" as if he had been strangled and

Diomedes became suspicious. Then I spoke: "Whether she is beautiful or not is none of your business, old man. She will never be one of the women on account of whom you will go to hell. She is an honest virgin, and will soon be an honest wife. Show us your gold. I am his best man and it is my task to help the young man... I am a Judaean citizen."

"He is a Galilean, is he not?" Your hair always gives you away. "Is he rich?"

"Yes, very."

We went downstairs then and Diomedes opened his coffers and treasure-chests. But tell the truth, John, did we not seem to be in Heaven with all the jewels and all the gold? Necklaces, wreaths, bracelets, ear-rings, hairnets of gold and precious stones, hairpins, buckles, rings... Ah! what magnificence! Haughtily, I picked up a necklace more or less like Aglae's. And rings, buckles, bracelets, everything like I had in my bag, and the same quantity. Diomedes was surprised and he kept asking: "What! Some more? But who is this man? And who is the bride? A princess?" When I had everything I wanted, I said: "The price?"

Oh! What a string of preparatory moaning on the times, taxes, risks, thieves! And another string of assurances on his honesty! And then his reply: "Just because it's you, I'll tell you the truth. Without exaggeration. But not even one penny less. I want twelve silver talents."

"Thief!" I said. And I went on: "Let's go, John. In Jerusalem we will find someone who is not such a thief as he is" and I pretended I was going out. He ran after me. "My great friend, my beloved friend, come, listen to your poor servant. I cannot accept less. It's impossible. Look. I'll make an effort at the cost of ruining myself. I'll do it because you have always honoured me with your friendship, and you made me do good business. Eleven talents, there you are. That is what I would pay if I had to buy that gold from someone starving. Not a penny less. It would be like bleeding my veins." Is that not what he said? He made me laugh and he disgusted me at the same time.

When I saw he was quite determined on the price, I pulled a fast one on him. "Dirty old rascal. Bear in mind that I do not want to buy, on the contrary, I want to sell. This is what I want to sell. Look. It is as beautiful as yours. Gold from Rome in the latest fashion. It will sell like hot cakes. You can have it for eleven talents. Exactly what you asked for yours. You fixed the price, and you pay." You should have heard him. "This is treachery! You betrayed the esteem I held you in! You want to ruin me! I cannot pay all that!" he shouted. "You appraised its value. So pay!" "I cannot." "Look, I'll take it to somebody else." "No, my friend, don't", and he stretched out his hooked hands towards Aglae's heap of gold. "Well, then, pay: I should ask for twelve talents. But I will be satisfied with the last price you asked." "I cannot." "Loan Shark! Look, I have a witness here and I can report you as a thief..." and I mentioned other virtues of his which I will not repeat on account of this boy...

At last, as I was anxious to sell and settle the matter quickly, I whispered something in his ear, something that I will not keep... What weight has a promise made to a thief? And I clenched the bargain at ten and a half. We came away whilst he was crying and offering his friendship and... women. And John was almost in tears. What does it matter if they think you are a depraved man! Nothing, providing you are not. Don't you know that the world is like that, and that you are a failure in the world? A young man who has not had any experience of women? Who do you think will believe you? Or if they believe you, well! I would not like them to think of me what they may think of you, if they believe you do not desire women.

Here, Master. Count them Yourself. I had a pile of coins. But I went to the excise man and I said to him: "Take this rubbish and give me the talents Isaac gave you." That was the last bit of information I got after closing the deal. But the last thing I said to Isaac-Diomedes was: "Remember that the Judas of the Temple exists no more. Now I am the disciple of a holy man. Pretend therefore that you never met me, if your life is dear to you." And I was on the point of wringing his neck because he gave me a sharp answer. '

'What did he say to you? 'Asks Simon, coldly.

'He said: "You, the disciple of a holy man? I will never believe it, or I will soon see your holy man here, asking for a woman." He said: "Diomedes is an old disgrace of the world. But you are a new one. And I may still change, because I became what I am when I was old. But you will not change. You were born like that." Filthy old man! He denies Your power, see? '

'And being a good Greek, he speaks the truth.'

'What do you mean, Simon? Are you referring to me? '

'No. I am referring to everyone. He is a man who knows gold and men's hearts the same way. He is a thief, the filthiest of all the filthy trades. But one perceives in him the philosophy of the great Greeks. He knows man, the animal with seven sinful jaws, the octopus that suffocates goodness, honesty, love and many other things, both in itself and in others. '

'But he does not know God. '

'And would you like to teach him? 'Asks Simon

'Yes, I would. Why? It's the sinners that need to know God. '

'True. But... the master must know Him to teach Him. '

'And do I not know Him? '

'Peace, My friends. The shepherds are coming. Do not let us upset their souls with our quarrels. Have you counted the money? That is enough. Fulfil all your actions as you fulfilled this one, and I repeat it once again, in future, if you can, do not tell lies, not even to accomplish a good deed. '

The shepherds come in.

'My friends. Here are ten and a half talents. The amount is short of one hundred coins which Judas has kept for the hotel expenses. Take them. '

'Are You giving them all?' Asks Judas.

'Yes, every penny. I do not want a farthing of that money. We have the offerings of God and of those who honestly seek God... and we will never lack what is necessary. Believe Me. Take the money and be happy, as I am, for the Baptist. Tomorrow, you will go towards his prison. Two of you: that is John and Matthias. Simeon and Joseph will go to Elias to report to him and to be taught for the future. Elias knows. Later, Joseph will come back with Levi. The meeting place, in ten days' time, is at the Fish Gate in Jerusalem, at sunrise. And now, let us eat and rest. Tomorrow, at dawn, I will leave with My disciples. I have nothing else to tell you for the time being. Later, you will hear from Me.'

And Jesus breaks the bread and passes it round.